# Ferdinand Tönnies on Public Opinion

## Selections and Analyses

Edited, Introduced, and Translated by
Hanno Hardt and Slavko Splichal

Foreword by Gary T. Marx

ROWMAN & LITTLEFIELD PUBLISHERS, INC.
*Lanham • Boulder • New York • Oxford*

ROWMAN & LITTLEFIELD PUBLISHERS, INC.

Published in the United States of America
by Rowman & Littlefield Publishers, Inc.
4720 Boston Way, Lanham, Maryland 20706
http://www.rowmanlittlefield.com

12 Hid's Copse Road, Cumnor Hill, Oxford OX2 9JJ, England

British Library Cataloguing in Publication Information Available

**Library of Congress Cataloging-in-Publication Data**

Tönnies, Ferdinand, 1855–1936.
    Ferdinand Tönnies on public opinion : selections and analyses / edited, introduced,
and translated by Hanno Hardt and Slavko Splichal.
        p. c.m.—(Critical media studies)
    Includes bibliographical references and index.
    ISBN 0-7425-0168-X (cloth ; alk.)—ISBN 0-7425-0169-8 (paper : alk.)
        1. Public opinion. I. Hardt, Hanno. II. Splichal, Slavko. III. Title. IV. Series.

HM1236 .T66 2000
303.3'8—dc21
                                                                        00-028061

Printed in the United States of America

∞™ The paper used in this publication meets the minimum requirements of
American National Standard for Information Sciences—Permanence of Paper
for Printed Library Materials, ANSI/NISO Z39.48-1992.

# Ferdinand Tönnies on Public Opinion

# CRITICAL MEDIA STUDIES:
## INSTITUTIONS, POLITICS, AND CULTURE

*Series Editor*

**Andrew Calabrese, University of Colorado at Boulder**

*Advisory Board*

## Titles in the Series

## Forthcoming in the Series

# Contents

# Acknowledgments

This book represents a collective effort to place the work of Ferdinand Tönnies in the early literature of communication and locate him among the primary theorists of public opinion. His work is part of the intellectual history of twentieth-century communication theory.

The translation and analysis of this remarkable historical document provide accessibility to his ideas of public opinion and present insights into the emergence of a new understanding of the power of the public at a time when the notion of public opinion gained prominence with the development of rapid means of communication in an urbanized and industrialized society.

The authors would like to thank Jan G. Tönnies for giving permission to translate selections from *Kritik der öffentlichen Meinung* and for providing the photographic images included in this book; Andrew Calabrese, series editor of Critical Media Studies, and Brenda Hadenfeldt of Rowman & Littlefield for their encouragement and support; and Gary T. Marx for providing a sociological context for an appraisal of Tönnies and his ideas on public opinion. The University of Iowa and the University of Ljubljana continue to offer a supportive work environment.

*Ferdinand Tönnies as a student. Photo courtesy of Christian Dahle.*

# Foreword

*Gary T. Marx*

What can you say about an under-read author who is prescient, sharply analytic, empirically observant, and deftly encyclopedic, who writes elegantly with a moral vision on issues that are more relevant today than they were when he wrote eighty years ago? Read him!

Ferdinand Tönnies is the kind of guy I would love to have met and learned from, whether in a European salon or an American saloon. As with the leading thinkers of his day, and in contrast to the narrowly specialized scholars of ours, he had an immense scholarly range from Greek and Latin and European history to knowledge of the contemporary thought of his day across a variety of social and cultural fields in Germany, as well as in France, England, and the United States.

Tönnies's enormous body of work is largely unknown to the English-speaking world. This is as true of his work on the media as his extensive writings on culture, religion, social movements, social ecology, social mores, and crime.[1] Indeed a recent bibliography lists more than nine hundred works, only a handful of which are available in English.[2]

Professors Hanno Hardt and Slavko Splichal have performed a useful service for students of the history of social thought, modernization, communication, public opinion, and critical media studies by making this work available in English, locating it contextually and adding fuller bibliographic references. They keep enough of Tönnies's original examples to give a sense of his style without overwhelming the reader with unfamiliar historical detail. Given the values of the Enlightenment and the ideals of the French Revolution, Tönnies asked (and joined) many of the right intellectual and moral questions. His answers in the form of richly illus-

1

trated classification schemes and a relatively coherent approach to public opinion are related to his broader conception of modern society.

Tönnies's knowledge of the natural sciences and his sure touch with metaphor and analogy make him a pleasure to read. He writes of bursting "opinion bubbles" and notes that "public opinion lacks a specific space and time. It spreads like a fog." He writes of the stream of anti-Semitic propaganda that "leaves its banks at times of public election," observes that "the press is free, but not its journalists," and draws on a reference to journalists as "prostitutes of the intellect."

He had an expansive conception of the factors that shaped and made up public opinion and the media. Here he is reminiscent of Erving Goffman, who urged us to see symbolic data everywhere. Beyond the usual mass media suspects, Tönnies looked for meaning in graffiti, posters, theater, hissing, applauding, and even raising flags and ringing bells as forms of demonstration. Understanding the mood of the people and the search for public opinion also required attending to the work of actors, painters, sculptors, architects, and musicians, all of which affect taste and opinions, if indirectly.

Consistent with scholars such as Max Weber, Emile Durkheim, and others who observed the transition from a more consensual traditional society to a more discordant urban-industrial one, he sought means to understand and channel social change of staggering magnitude. And consistent with the social control/guidance concerns of early twentieth-century sociologists such as Edward A. Ross in the United States, public opinion was seen as an important mechanism for this.

The concepts for which he is best known in English are of course community and society (*Gemeinschaft* and *Gesellschaft*), which are differentiated partly by their mode of communication—traditional, handed-down beliefs are characteristic of community, whereas public opinion is more rationally and scientifically based and grows out of reflection and discussion typical of society.

Tönnies used the central concept of public opinion and related forms to generate a way of thinking about societies and social change that is still useful. Further, unlike most contemporary scholars, he joined intellectual and moral questions and believed that normative ideals could be found within the empirical. He was hopeful that under the right conditions (i.e., as practiced by the well-educated and as divorced from one-sided and self-interested media accounts), public opinion would serve as a guide for social betterment. He appreciated the intimate and intricate link between public opinion and democracy.

In Tönnies's usage an opinion expressed in public is not public opinion. Nor are opinion polls, which reveal many publics with diverse opinions, the same thing as general public opinion. The latter is defined by its con-

Tönnies hoped that the media, by effecting a genuine public opinion, might help restore valuable elements of the community type of society to modern society. He would have been disappointed to see that, with the help of scientific and technological elites, the media had instead moved even further, if more subtly, in the dependent and manipulative directions of which he was critical.

The public created by the mass media is a relatively passive recipient of information and instructions rather than an active participant. This is far from the concept of an active public opinion as envisioned by eighteenth-century theorists and as implied by the interaction of well-informed citizens in a New England town meeting.

Several decades ago, with network television and a shrinking press, the trend toward public passivity accelerated. However, with new interactive media, whether cable television and its variants, forms of remote communication, or the Internet (with its lower cost, logistical advantages of time, place, and accessibility, and "many-to-many" communication) the issue is dynamic and offers rich possibilities for study and perhaps even reason for a little optimism.

Whatever the contemporary scoreboard, for democratic social change and a better understanding of public opinion and the media, it is vital to raise the kinds of broad normative and research questions that Tönnies addresses. While it is unlikely any scholar will ever be capable of filling his shoes, we would do well to follow in his footsteps.

## NOTES

1. On crime, for example, see Mathieu Deflem, "Ferdinand Tönnies on Crime and Society: An Unexplored Contribution to Criminological Sociology," *History of the Human Sciences* 12, no. 3 (1999): 87-116.

2. Rolf Fechner, *Ferdinand Tönnies: Werverzeichnis* (Berlin: Walter de Gruyter, 1992), as cited in Deflem.

3. Among early works in this tradition for example, Herbert Blumer, "Collective Behavior," in *New Outline of the Principles of Sociology*, ed. Albert M. Lee (New York: Barnes & Noble, 1957); Kurt Lang and Gladys Lang, *Collective Dynamics* (New York: Crowell, 1961); Orrin Klapp, *Currents of Unrest: An Introduction to Collective Behavior* (New York: Holt, Rinehart, and Winston, 1972); Ralph Turner and Lewis Killian, *Collective Behavior*, 3d ed. (Englewood Cliffs, N.J.: Prentice-Hall, 1987); Gary T. Marx and D. McAdam, *Collective Behavior and Social Movements Process and Structure* (Englewood Cliffs, N.J.: Prentice-Hall, 1994).

4. Institute for Propaganda Analysis, Albert M. Lee, and Elizabeth Lee, *The Fine Art of Propaganda: A Study of Father Coughlin's Speeches* (New York: Harcourt, Brace, 1939); Leo Lowenthal and Norman Guterman, *Prophets of Deceit: A Study of the Techniques of the American Agitator* (New York: Harper, 1949).

# Part I
# Introduction and Analyses

"believing pertains to the heart, and opining to the head." The relationship of "public—opinion" and "public—public opinion," respectively, at that time had already become a matter of dispute among American political scientists.[1]

During the next decades the list of controversial questions was remarkably extended. If we do not want to relinquish the idea of public opinion, we have to reconcile ourselves to the fact that a *universal* definition of the public and public opinion cannot be attained. The reason does not lie primarily in the existence of too many exclusive definitions (which would render impossible the formulation of an "average definition" or the establishment of a "common denominator") but derives instead from contradictions inherent in the very concept of "public opinion." While a universal definition of public opinion clearly does not exist, the question of whether public opinion itself exists is more controversial: a number of authors would undoubtedly "subscribe" to Pierre Bourdieu's ([1972] 1979) famous slogan that "public opinion does not exist," but many others would strongly disagree.

Central to the normative concept of public opinion is the principle of *publicity*. Modern democracy is usually thought of as a product of the Enlightenment, which raised the idea of publicity to a fundamental moral principle. In his treatise "To Perpetual Peace" Immanuel Kant ([1795] 1983) suggests that the principle of publicity is the fundamental and universal principle of human public agency. But it is Jeremy Bentham who should be credited for the first in-depth discussion of the relationship between public opinion and the principle of publicity, including the definition of the latter as the foundation of public opinion and people's sovereignty. In contemporary (deliberative) democracies, the idea of publicity primarily refers to the public sphere, in which the "public use of reason" or "public discussion" of free and equal citizens can (or ought to) take place and public opinion is formed and expressed.

Ever since the Enlightenment, public opinion has bestowed an aura of legitimacy upon laws, policies, decisions, convictions, or even wars, often for manipulative purposes: actions and beliefs appear justified or valid if they are in accordance with "public opinion." Bryce ([1888] 1995) identifies government by public opinion as one of three fundamental forms of popular government, in addition to government by a plenary assembly of citizens and by representative systems. He argues that government by public opinion could be considered an attempt to apply government by the plenary assembly to a large population or to modify the representative system (cf. Tönnies 1922, 323). While premodern states legitimized their origins and developments by insisting on the divine will, modern democracies largely refer to public opinion. The latter is indispensable for the legitimacy of governments that claim that their power is based on the consent of the governed. In this sense, the functional equivalence of religion and public opinion is obvious, according to Tönnies. Such "legitimization pressure" can partly explain why the public and public opinion are so differently—even controversially—defined, interpreted, and constantly appealed to but often ignored in practice.

Consequently, Walter Lippmann writes in the early 1920s that "since Public Opinion is supposed to be the prime mover in democracies, one might reasonably expect to find a vast literature. One does not find it. . . . The existence of the force called Public Opinion is in the main taken for granted" ([1922] 1960, 253). The main reason for his disillusionment lies in the fact that since the earliest dissertations on public opinion in the eighteenth century, "'public opinion' [has taken the form of] a political or ideological construct, rather than a discrete sociological referent" (Baker 1990, 172). Despite an earlier disenchantment—at the end of the eighteenth century—regarding the omnipotence of the public and public opinion, efforts to (re)discover the discrete sociological referent of public opinion have been primarily associated with twentieth-century sociological thought. However, the results of these efforts remain controversial.

For instance, the semantic heterogeneity of concepts like public, publicness, publicity, and public opinion over time and across disciplines—which challenges their validity—is closely related to their frequent use in the most diverse theories. Also, the symptomatic referral to an extensive literature on the public and public opinion in dissertations since the beginning of the second half of the twentieth century has never yielded a clear and unequivocal definition of these concepts. As Harwood Childs concludes in his survey of definitions of public opinion, "there are about as many definitions as there are studies in the field" (1939, 327).

Such difficulties led Childs (1965) and many others—among them V. O. Key ([1961] 1967), Benjamin Ginsberg (1986), James Beniger (1987), and John Zaller (1992)[2]—to conclude that perhaps the best way out of the growing perplexities would be to substitute the term "mass opinion" for "public opinion" in empirical research. Earlier, Newcomb (1950, 176) had suggested the term "group attitudes" as more appropriate for naming the subject of "public opinion" surveys. The pursuit of empirical inquiries into an operational definition did not solve the problem, however; Philip Converse is among a few authors who are convinced that "the firm establishment of a public opinion polling industry . . . homogenized the definition and stabilized it for [the] foreseeable future" (1987, 13). The facts, however, prove the opposite: despite enormous amounts of money and attention devoted to public opinion polling, there are "few theoretical perspectives to guide research on the role of public sentiment in the political process. Perhaps this lack is not so surprising, given that even consistent definitions of the concept 'public opinion' are missing" (Glynn and McLeod 1984, 43). This conceptual perplexity—which resulted in the absence of an agreed-upon definition of public opinion—is not specific to public opinion, however. There is abundant evidence that "from the beginning of modern social science, there has been sharp disagreement on most of the questions it has considered" (Wilson 1962, 74).

Not surprisingly, understandings and attempts at defining the public and public opinion are often motivated by (political) interests, common-sense myopia, or theoretical exclusivism. Thus the proposal that "true" social scientists abandon the use of a concept with such unstandardized meanings is understandable. As early as the beginning of this century the definitional issue had become so confounding that a 1924 round table on political statistics at the U.S. National Conference on the Science of Politics concluded that it would be wise to "avoid the use of the term public opinion, if possible" (Binkley 1928, 389). Half a century later, Luhmann (1971, 339–401) argued that the classical concept of the public was "too undetermined" and an "inappropriate category" for analytical and critical purposes and thus merely an "agrarian-historic concept" without reference to practical existence or practical object. Public opinion supposedly degenerated into an "inner media" of the political system, a mirror "generated by mass media to regulate the watching of the observers." With its help, politicians observe one another, their adversaries, and ordinary people, who are mere observers (Luhmann 1994, 63). In the same vein, Bourdieu ([1972] 1979) entitled his resounding rejection "Public Opinion Doesn't Exist" to express a similar disbelief in the validity of the concept.

The increasing number of treatises on public opinion certainly did not decrease the opacity of the concept, but this argument should not be sufficient to renounce the concept itself. At least two reasons speak against it. First, although the theoretical concept of public opinion is recognized only in the modern age of parliamentary democracies, its conceptual dimensions reach back to more remote historical periods. In other words, the concept veils a more universal validity than the one conferred on it by bourgeois society. For instance, as Negt (1980) and Beaud and Kaufmann (1999) argue, it is unduly restricted by Habermas (1992a, 465) when he claims that the idea of the public sphere *(Öffentlichkeit)* should not be extended into the sixteenth and seventeenth centuries, since that would substantially change the meaning of the concept. In contrast to Habermas—and with reference to Margaret Mead's ([1937] 1965) discussion—Beaud admonishes that even in primitive communities anthropologists have discovered mechanisms of group interaction that advance processes of differentiation in which we could recognize "the individualistic definition of public opinion in which liberalism would like to see the foundations of modern democratic societies alone" (1993, 125). A case in point is the ancient Greek city-state, in which citizens directly participated in state (political, public) affairs—basically in the sense of a specific "realm of social life in which something approaching public opinion can be formed" and in which "access is guaranteed to all citizens."

Second, despite the lack of a clear, unambiguous definition, public opinion was typically institutionalized in modern societies, essentially in three distinct nationwide[3] forms, although none of them genuinely represented an ideally defined public. In operational terms at least, public opinion is expressed and/or (re)presented in, or by, parliaments, mass media, and polling. Regardless of whether public opinion was considered as originating from rational discussion (or merely as a widespread diffusion of elite opinion, even by coercion) or whether it presupposed the public either as a corporate social entity or merely a (statistical) aggregation of individuals or without any specific actor, it was always assumed that public opinion is (at least) *publicly expressed* opinion, which—in some way—*represents* the will of the (majority of) people or citizenry. Yet even this least common denominator was dissolved by the rise of polling in the 1930s, when public *expression* was replaced by public *presentation* of data.

The fact that *parliament* generally may be called an "organ of opinion of the public" reflects a widely held assumption advocated by normative political theories and early sociological theorizing of public opinion (notably by American pragmatism in the work of Park and Dewey—and Tönnies). However, representative government (including "government by public opinion") has never been a system in which parliamentary representatives had to regard opinions of the electorate; it has never been a direct form of popular sovereignty. Rather, since its foundation, representative government—even if based on the principle of universal suffrage—has been rule by elites, distinguished from the majority of citizens by social status, education, particularistic interests, and way of life.

Since the first modern newspapers, the *mass media* have played an important role in conceptualizations of public opinion. They deliver not only information to the public (and thus are an important element in the process of public opinion *formation*), but they are also the main means of *expression* of the public, constituting a kind of "virtual" or "imagined" public. In addition, the press and other media represent a "general medium" for more restricted means of expression, like associations, meetings, or demonstrations. The media not only express but also influence public opinion. In their discussions of public opinion, Tönnies, Dewey, and Lippmann considered newspapers more important than other forms of public, political organization. Yet the press was neither regarded as an organ of public opinion nor deemed identical to it; it figured primarily as an organ of political parties and commercial corporations.

*Public opinion polling* developed during the decline of the (idea of) rational public and has been considered the first "scientific mastering" of public opinion during the last fifty years, when it was institutionalized in Western democracies. Formerly the social sciences had attempted, rather unsuccessfully, a scientific operationalization of the normative concepts of public opinion, but with polling (as its prophets believed) they seemed to have achieved a satisfactory degree of empirical validity. Moreover, media owners and news workers soon became aware of the importance of polling as a competitive form of institutionalizing public opinion and adopted "scientific" polls widely. Yet similarly to press and parliament, polling was also soon criticized for its negative effects on public opinion and democratic life, and it was "accused" of antidemocratic manipulation and control over public opinion.

Classical liberal theories of the reign of public opinion were advanced during the Enlightenment, for the most part in England and France, and with some delay in Germany. They emerged from a utilitarian theory of a free press that was promulgated by James Mill and Jeremy Bentham, who saw in public opinion the emergence of reasoned individuals against absolutist authority (Wilson 1962, 208; Keane 1992, 66–71). To this end, autonomy, competence, morality, and responsibility for the common good are demanded of the individual. And it is no coincidence that these qualities materialized in the nascent bourgeoisie, since the origins and the disintegration of the liberal public are connected to the development of capitalism. In terms of a strict (liberal-bourgeois or Enlightenment) definition, however, it is only possible to speak of public opinion and the public in England and France at the end of the seventeenth century and eighteenth centuries, respectively.

Bentham conceived of publicity as a necessary precondition "for putting the tribunal of the public in a condition for forming an enlightened judgment" ([1791] 1994, 590). He saw in the principle of publicity a safeguard for public *confidence* in the assembly and an assurance that the latter would perform its duties. Bentham emphasized the importance of general *visibility* and *accessibility*, which ought to enable efficient *control* over power elites. Similarly to the disciplinary technology on which he elaborated in *The Panopticon Writings* ([1787] 1995), Bentham related the principle of publicity to a "system of distrust" and argued that "every good political institution is founded upon this base."

In Bentham's understanding of publicity, the aspect of rational debate was only of secondary importance—in sharp contrast to political-philosophical dissertations during the Enlightenment that considered public opinion a political phenomenon of prime importance, bringing to the forefront the relationship between citizens and authorities. For instance, Jean Jacques Rousseau's ([1762] 1947) "model" of public opinion was based on the absolute sovereignty of the people as a community of equal citizens (irrespective of their status, property, etc.) within the nation-state.

Generally, public opinion was supposed to secure a liberal form of government and represent "the government of the government," as William A. MacKinnon ([1828] 1971, 9) suggested in the first monograph ever written on public opinion.

MacKinnon's comprehensive work, published in 1828—the first one entirely devoted to the "rise, progress, and present state of public opinion," as indicated by the subtitle—concluded the "prehistorical" period of public opinion. Like Bentham, MacKinnon distinguishes among three social classes which, in his case, are entirely based on wealth because "where freedom and civilization exist, wealth is so entirely the only power either to individuals or to government, that no other means or choice is left of distinguishing the several classes of society, than by the property of the individuals of which they are formed" ([1828] 1971, 2). Using statistical criteria, MacKinnon divides society into (1) the upper class, consisting of those who "have the means of constantly supporting one hundred, or any greater number of men, fit for labour," (2) the middle class, consisting of individuals who are able to support from two to one hundred working men, and (3) the lower class, which consists of all others.

Historically, the creation of public opinion must meet four fundamental conditions: (1) an increase of the power of machinery, (2) communication (transportation) facilities, (3) proper religious feeling, and (4) spread of information through society (improved systems of education, press). These conditions are linked to the development and relative growth of the middle class and, to a lesser degree, the upper class, whose size is strictly limited in free countries by a growing middle class. Thus MacKinnon was the first to systematically formulate certain sociological assumptions about the (political) function of public opinion and to advance a thesis connecting public opinion and the middle class.

He emphasized that the power of public opinion primarily depends on the proportion that the upper and middle classes of society bear to the lower class. According to MacKinnon, the size of the middle-and upper-class population relative to lower class determines "the quantity of intelligence and wealth that exists in the community" ([1828] 1971, 15). He also suggests that "popular clamour is powerful in proportion as the lower class is ignorant and numerous" and relies on the ignorance and prejudice of the uneducated. But the fundamental characteristic of public opinion is that it is well-informed and intelligent. He continues, "Public opinion may be said to be, that sentiment on any given subject which is entertained by the best informed, most intelligent, and most moral persons in the community, which is gradually spread and adopted by nearly all persons of any education or proper feeling in a civilized state."

The increase in the power of public opinion, according to MacKinnon, is closely related to the development of liberal government: "This seems to prove that public opinion secures a liberal form of government, not that a government secures public opinion" ([1828] 1971, 9). This is similar to what Edmund Burke had written before him: "Let us give a faithful pledge to the people, that we honor, indeed, the crown, but that we belong to them; that we are their auxiliaries, and not their task-masters" ([1769] 1967, 212). MacKinnon emphasizes that "to follow, not to force, the public inclination; to give a direction, a form, a technical dress, and a specific sanction to the general sense of the community is the true end of legislature," and that in a civilized country the government is governed by public opinion and must follow its dictates; it would be an error to imagine that the government can command public opinion, apart from shorter periods of despotic governments. Wilson (1962, 34) even generalizes the early liberal belief that public opinion creates an obligation for public servants to follow "one of the converging ideas in the theory of public opinion," although the controversies throughout the twentieth century indicate that such a convergence never existed.

Rousseau's *Social Contract* ([1762] 1947) represents a kind of constitution of the Enlightenment. According to Wilhelm Bauer ([1933] 1963, 669), Rousseau—with his concept of *volonté générale*—expanded on Montesquieu's *esprit général* while both were heirs to Locke's attempts to supply a legal and ethical orientation for the phenomenon of public opinion, called "the law of opinion and reputation." The guiding question of Rousseau's reflections is how to attain a reliable, legal government with justice and legality in harmony. The social contract solves the problem of finding a common defense and protection of personality and property; at the same time, each individual would be united with all others while remaining free and subordinated only to himself. The solution lies in the subordination of each individual to the supreme leadership of the general will, which emerges with the assimilation of individuals into a collective moral body whose political form is the republic. Rousseau emphasizes that only the general will *(la volonté générale)* can lead the powers of the country in accordance with reasonable common welfare—the reason for its creation. The general will—which exists only in the search for a universal good—materializes in the law, which is equally valid for everyone and must be distinguished from the will of everyone *(la volonté de tous)*. The latter is only the sum of individual desires and expresses private interests—it is a difference between normative and empirical collective wills. Only in an ideal situation do these two wills coincide, provided that individuals subject themselves to a general law; then a popular vote becomes identical with the general will.

Rousseau adds a fourth type of law to the categories of political, citizenship, and penal laws to guarantee the execution of other laws—"manners and morals, customs, and more than all, of *opinions*" ([1762] 1947, 113;

emphasis added); it is not a special type of law and for that reason is the most important of all. However, he does not make a precise distinction between the general will and public opinion. The general will expresses itself through laws, whereas public opinion is the judgment of the people, which is expressed in censorship; it is thus "the kind of law of which the censor is the minister, and which he only causes to be applied to particular cases, after the example of the prince." The general will is based on the debates and decisions of "appropriately educated people" and is expressed as general opinion, whereas special opinion (the opinion of special groups) prevails at times when the general will does not exist. The general will is always correct; it is only the capacity of its guiding judgment that is not always sufficiently enlightened.

On their own people will always want the good, but they will not always see the good and may need to be directed, led—in short, enlightened—sometimes also with the help of censorship.[4] Public opinion as general opinion is based (and here Rousseau resembles Montaigne) on moral authority and therefore comes close to the role of moral arbiter (Tönnies 1922, 291). In other words, public opinion would have an emphatic function (of social control) as well as a legislative function (Vreg 1980, 44). Rousseau was convinced that the general will could only be expressed if there were no special interest groups in society—which would be concerned with their own interests[5]—and if every citizen reasoned with his own mind. Public debate and argument were almost superfluous: the general will is more a consensus of hearts than of arguments presented in a public discussion; publicity is reduced to a discussion of public affairs in public assemblies. There is no specific organ that forms the general will; the government is merely an administrative committee.

Whereas the principle of publicity had an instrumental function for utilitarians—and even a disciplinarian role for Bentham—Kant lifts it to a transcendent principle mediating between politics and morals in public law. Unlike Rousseau, Kant does not believe that man is by nature good (yet he was grateful to Rousseau for helping him overcome his own blind dismissal of the illiterate masses and setting him on the path toward respect for human beings and their rights). Thus Kant does not defend the principle of publicity primarily for the sake of moral improvement but argues that it is necessary to use this "mechanism of nature" as a means to creating a legal maxim that people would obey. In his treatise "To Perpetual Peace" Kant advances *the transcendental formula* of public justice: "'All actions that affect the rights of other men are wrong if their maxim is not consistent with publicity.' This principle is to be considered not only ethical . . . but also juridical" ([1795] 1983, 135). Without the possibility of publicity and without the principle of public agency, there would be no justice. The reverse is also true: if a goal can only be achieved with the help of publicity, it also means no distrust in the underlying political maxims that are congruent with the goals and rights of all. Publicity alone, therefore, can guarantee harmony between politics and morals: it guarantees legal order while fulfilling an enlightened role. Enlightenment, according to Kant's essay "What Is Enlightenment," is liberation from the human impossibility of using one's own reason without being guided by someone else. ("Have the courage to use your *own* reason is the motto of Enlightenment!") Enlightened opinion endowed with publicity and scholarly prudence are, according to Kant, the most reliable sources of human progress.

Kant's principle of publicity is not directly connected to public opinion but rather to the reconciliation of politics with morals and the achievement of consensus; yet his notion of publicity comes very close to the idea of public opinion when he relates it to the mutual "agreement of all judgments with each other." However, Kant ([1781] 1952) specifically elaborates the concept of *opinion* which, in his *Critique of Pure Reason*, is defined as the lowest level of "holding for true" (*Fürwahrhalten*).

Kant's conceptualization of holding for true is the basis for Ferdinand Tönnies's notion of opinion in his *Kritik der öffentlichen Meinung*. Holding for true is, according to Kant, determined by the subjective and objective validity of judgment and has three levels: opining (*Meinen*), believing (*Glauben*), and knowing (*Wissen*). Opinion is both subjectively (for myself) and objectively (for everyone) insufficient; belief is subjectively sufficient but lacks objectivity; only knowledge is sufficient on both accounts. Yet one must never dare to put forth even a mere opinion without some knowledge; thus an opinion is never merely an "arbitrary fiction." One cannot possibly hold opinions in judgments of pure reason. It would be absurd, for example, to have an opinion about pure mathematics—in such a field, one must either *know* or abstain from forming a judgment altogether.

Hegel's analysis of public opinion, published in *Grundlinien einer Philosophie des Rechts* ([1821] 1971), emerges from his understanding of the freedom of will, which ran counter to liberal thinking. Human freedom is not arbitrary. It presupposes a rationally organized state with laws and institutions that are respected by individuals in their activities. By doing so, individuals first and foremost respond to demands put forth by the state in terms of the "substantive and particular interest" of all concerned (Schacht 1972, 322).

In contrast to Bentham, for example, who sees in the principle of publicity a safeguard for public confidence in the assembly and an assurance that the assembly would perform its duties, Hegel defends the publicity of the estates debates in Germany primarily on the grounds of expanding knowledge of public affairs among the general population. Publicizing debates should enable public opinion to gain insight into problems as well as obtain reliable information needed to make rational judgments. At the same time, public opinion ought to "learn to respect the work, abilities, virtues, and dexterity of ministers and officials." Publicity, according to Hegel, is an "antidote to the self-conceit of individuals singly and *en masse*" and the "chief means of their education" ([1821] 1971, 203–204, sec. 315). Such a functional definition of publicity is, to a large degree, indebted to Hegel's definition of the role of estates as the mediating organ that stands "between the government in general on the one hand and the nation broken up into particulars (people and associations) on the other." In contrast to the liberal belief that the government has to follow public opinion, Hegel considers the estates to be the mediator and reductor of both the power of the crown and the particular interests of individuals and associations. He also views estates as the bulwark against "an unorganized opinion and volition . . . in opposition to the organized state" ([1821] 1971, 197, sec. 302).

Contrary to the business of the state—in which only those with "qualifications and disposition that accord with this end" (above all, knowledge, understanding, and property) can participate—the sphere of public opinion is a field that "is open to everyone to express one's purely personal political opinions and make them count" (Hegel [1821] 1971, 201, sec. 308–309). "Public opinion is the unorganized way in which a people's opinions and wishes are made known," as Gans summarizes Hegel's lecture (Add. sec. 316). Within public opinion, two different strands are ceaselessly interwoven: public usage and the authority of reason, and contingency, ignorance, and faulty reasoning. According to Hegel,

> the formal subjective freedom of individuals consists in their having and expressing their own private judgments, opinions, and recommendations on affairs of state. This freedom is collectively manifested in what is called "public opinion," in which what is absolutely universal, the substantive and true, is linked with its opposite, the purely particular and private opinions of the Many. Public opinion as it exists is thus a standing self-contradiction, knowledge as appearance, the essential just as directly present as the inessential. ([1821] 1971, 204, sec. 316)

The contradictory status of public opinion in Hegel's theory is partly related to the "disorganization of civil society," as Habermas argues ([1962] 1995, 119). But more than that, with Hegel's conceptualization we first encounter the inherent contradiction in the character of public opinion. In later developments, this contradictory nature would become even more evident with authors who criticized the tyranny of the majority (e.g., Alexis de Tocqueville, John Stuart Mill, and James Bryce).

Karl Marx vigorously criticized Hegel's theory of estates in his *Critique of Hegel's Philosophy of Right* ([1843] 1974), arguing that it is not the state, as Hegel asserts, but rather civil society *(bürgerliche Gesellschaft)* that is the key to understanding historical developments. But he basically did not deviate from Hegel's controversial concept of public opinion. Similar to Hegel, Marx argues for publicity and freedom of the press, most explicitly in "Die Verhandlungen des 6. rheinischen Landtags" (The debates of the sixth provincial assembly of the Rhineland), published as a six-part series in the *Rheinische Zeitung* of May 1842. For Marx, publicity is a precondition for a functioning political assembly because a "truly political assembly only prospers under the great protectorate of public spirit, as the living [prospers] only under the protectorate of a *clear air*" ([1842] 1969, 65). Parliamentary freedom, which had been defended by certain representatives of the estates as superior to press freedom, according to Marx, is either privilege or censorship. And while it may have been the freedom of pre-Revolutionary French assemblies, Marx introduces the time of publicness not in the sense of truthful reporting to the public, however, but in the sense of being reported to a genuine public; in other words, not an "imaginary reading public" but a "living current public" ([1842] 1969, 62). That is why the publication of provincial parliamentary debates in official newspapers only—a form of censorship performed by the estates—was worse than no publication at all. Censorship is criticism reduced to a monopoly in the hands of authority which, because of its secrecy, loses its rationality. However, the substance of freedom of the press stems precisely from criticism and the "sharp knife of reason." Therefore, what is needed are not laws regulating censorship but laws regulating the press. With press laws, it is freedom that penalizes, whereas with censorship laws—which are only laws formally because they do not express the vital laws of human activities—it is freedom that is penalized. "The press law is thus a legal recognition of freedom of the press. It is the law because it is a positive existence of freedom" (Marx [1842] 1969, 77).

Marx noticed a new kind of nascent censorship in the large cash deposits that the state required from publishers prior to publication. He also placed the kind of press freedom favored by representatives of the bourgeoisie in the sphere of material censorship. Marx criticized the economic subordination of the press to capital, based on the presupposition of the formal-legal freedom of the press—a position later also proclaimed by Lippmann. Marx's critique rests on the experiences of the contemporary French press, an issue also debated by the provincial assembly of the Rhineland, which ultimately characterized the French press as being "too free." His opinion was just the opposite (Splichal 1981, 104). Marx demonstrated that the interest of the bourgeoisie is not to eliminate entirely unfreedom of the press but only to replace a certain kind of unfreedom—censorship as a kind of external unfreedom—which limits the free availability of property in the sphere of the press by another, inner unfreedom. For representatives of the bourgeoisie it is a case of "classic incongruity" if the sphere of the press is exempted from the general freedom of entrepreneurship (Marx [1842] 1969, 88). Yet if freedom of the press is based on free enterprise, it becomes just another privilege—not the right of a human being or a citizen but merely the right of the owner. Would it, therefore, not be better to treat entrepreneurial freedom as a kind of press freedom? Absurdity is present in both examples. Of course, the press is also a business, although in this case it is not a matter of writers but printers and publishers, which raises a yet completely different set of questions. This is why Marx ([1842] 1969, 92) emphasizes that "the first freedom of the press is that it is not a business."

While theories of the rule of public opinion from Burke to Rousseau attribute sovereignty to public opinion and to the public itself, the public as the materialized form of the principle of publicity has always been either implicitly or explicitly limited by the competence of individuals. As such, it is efficiently institutionalized in the political system of the bourgeois legal state that represents the beginning of a gradual disintegration of the classical bourgeois public. As Habermas says,

> the principle of publicity based on the public of educated people who reason and enjoy art and the medium of bourgeois press—which, at the beginning, undoubtedly had a critical function against the secret practice of the absolutist state and was consolidated in the methods of organs of the legal state—has been refunctioned for demonstrative and manipulative purposes. ([1965] 1980, 10)

The concept of the rule of public opinion would soon become the object of severe criticism. The period of confidence in public opinion—based on the belief in the moral judgment of the common man (middle class) proclaimed in the age of Enlightenment—would be followed by a period of distrust in his capabilities and competence. Doubts were first clearly expressed by Hegel and followed in the mid-1800s by political-philosophical critiques of the tyranny of public opinion, which continued to dominate the period to the rise of sociopsychological positivism and empiricism emerging in the early 1900s.

The liberalist theory of the tyranny of public opinion began to take shape in the middle of the nineteenth century, during a period when democracy was expanding to embrace all social classes. At first glance, this new school of thought does not seem to differ substantially from classical liberal theory. Here too questions about the possibility of rational debate among an educated public took center stage along with the historical limitations of the formation of public opinion into a specific social category—the bourgeois public. According to Mill ([1859] 1985, 81), the latter was composed of the white population in the United States and represented by the middle class in England—from which "many foolish individuals" were excluded. The essential distinction was to be found in the explicit social limitation of the public to the wisest individuals; it emerges from the critique of a utilitarian theory of freedom of the press and is a consequence of a different conceptualization of the function of public opinion. In contrast to the classic understanding, public opinion is no longer understood as a means of freedom and democracy but rather as tyranny over reason. For John Stuart Mill ([1859] 1985, 131), the purpose of press freedom is not to guarantee happiness for the greatest number of people—as it was for Bentham—but rather the pursuit of Truth. The latter is rarely identical with the opinion of the many or the opinion of the masses, which represents "collective mediocrity." Such freedom can only be enjoyed by a mature society rather than by a society in which people are becoming ever more similar and therefore more mediocre—as Tocqueville ([1840] 1995) observes about France—and in which the task of the elite must be to limit the excessive power of public opinion. Public opinion, because of its complete domination, is more than anything else the cause for a general similarity of people; like Christian morals, it requires, above all, obedience and dictates what individuals can and must or must not do. This modified conceptualization of public opinion was certainly linked to historical changes, inspiring Mill to say that "the time, it is to be hoped, is gone by, when any defense would be necessary of the 'liberty of the press' as one of the securities against corrupt or tyrannical government" ([1859] 1985, 75).

According to Tocqueville, the greatest dangers to the American republic emanated from the omnipotence of the majority. He was convinced that the supremacy of the majority was so strong that

> freedom of opinion does not exist in America. The Inquisition has never been able to prevent a vast number of anti-religious books from circulating in Spain. The empire of the majority succeeds much better in the United States, since it actually removes any wish to publish them. ([1840] 1995, 1: chap. 15)

The domination of the majority, not unlike a rigid social or caste system, produces silence and the impossibility of change. Thus the society most favorable to the "great revolutions of the mind" is one in which there is neither complete equality of the entire community nor absolute separation of social classes. Tocqueville suggests that

> whenever social conditions are equal, public opinion presses with enormous weight upon the minds of each individual; it surrounds, directs, and oppresses him; and this arises from the very constitution of society much more than from its political laws. As men grow more alike, each man feels himself weaker in regard to all the rest; as he discerns nothing by which he is considerably raised

above them or distinguished from them, he mistrusts himself as soon as they assail him. Not only does he mistrust his strength, but he even doubts of his right; and he is very near acknowledging that he is in the wrong, when the greater number of his countrymen assert that he is so. The majority do not need to force him; they convince him. ([1840] 1995, 2: sec. 3, chap. 21)

According to Tocqueville, it is essential for a truly democratic system that the legislative power be so constituted as to represent the majority without necessarily being "the slave of its passions." In addition, the legislative, executive, and judiciary powers should be separated and mutually independent. In such circumstances, Tocqueville believed, a government could be formed that would still be democratic and yet not endangered by the tyranny of the majority.

In the aftermath of the bourgeois revolutions of the eighteenth and nineteenth centuries, the actual reduction of the public to the bourgeois class effectively means the narrowing of the social category of the public and its closure to the emerging working class. The theoretical arguments of Tocqueville, Mill, and Bryce only legitimize the process. Whereas the liberal-democratic concept of public opinion is critically aimed against absolutist authority, the revised theory of public opinion in the period of the consolidation of the rule of law attempts to legitimize and conserve the economic and political powers of the bourgeois class against the masses. In *Liberty,* Mill even advocates despotism as a legitimate mode of government in dealing with "barbarians," while at the same time he sees in public opinion a great danger to modern democracies.

> The modern regime of public opinion is, in an unorganized form, what the Chinese educational and political systems are in an organized; and unless individuality shall be able successfully to assert itself against the yoke, Europe, notwithstanding its noble antecedents and its professed Christianity, will tend to become another China. ([1859] 1985, 138)

Just as the early liberal period—which champions the rule of public opinion—concluded with MacKinnon's (1828) comprehensive work, the period of a liberal critique of the tyranny of the majority and public opinion reached its zenith in the work of James Bryce at the end of the nineteenth century. His thorough discussion of public opinion in *The American Commonwealth,* published in 1888, uses the United States as an example of the inexpedient "government by public opinion" in which "the wishes and views of the people prevail, even before they have been conveyed through the regular law-appointed organs, and without the need of their being so conveyed" ([1888] 1995, 925).

Public opinion is expressed through four main organs: the press, public meetings (primarily during election campaigns), elections, and citizen associations. Among them, Bryce considers newspapers the most important organs because they, "as narrators, as advocates, and as weathercocks," not only report events but also advance arguments and mirror public opinion. Although none of these instruments can provide a constant, instant, and reliable estimate of public opinion, politicians—who do not differ from their constituents in regard to their virtues and ideas—act as if such an instrument existed: they "look incessantly for manifestations of current popular opinion, and . . . shape their course in accordance with their reading of those manifestations" ([1888] 1995, 920). An active monitoring of public opinion would become critical, particularly with V. O. Key's definition, in later conceptualizations of public opinion.

Yet Bryce argues that the absence of a reliable means of ascertaining public opinion, or the will of the majority, is less important than the danger that "minorities may not sufficiently assert themselves" because of widespread pressures of the majority in all spheres of public life, both inside and outside of legislation. He was the first to identify—in addition to the tyranny of the majority discussed by Tocqueville[6]—the phenomena of a passive "silent majority" and the "fatalism of the multitude," which, together with the former, makes the decisive role of public opinion particularly questionable. On the other hand, Bryce also reveals the paradox that the uneducated, humbler classes differ in opinion from the educated and propertied classes. Despite the fact that there is little substance in the beliefs of "the man in the car," he argues that the humbler classes "have often been proved by the event to have been right and their so-called betters wrong" ([1888] 1995, 913). Nevertheless, he clearly takes up the position typically expressed by Edmund Burke and later by Tocqueville and Mill who, as Wilson (1962, 213) argues, could not "realize that the minority can be even more tyrannical than the majority." Bryce suggests that

> the duty, therefore, of a patriotic statesman in a country where public opinion rules, would seem rather to resist and correct than to encourage the dominant sentiment. . . . In a nation with a keen moral sense and a capacity for strong emotions, opinion based on a love of what is deemed just or good will resist the multitude when bent on evil. ([1888] 1995, 921)

"Vigorous individuality" and a "keen moral sense" of citizens brought about by appropriate socialization would be the only safeguards against majority pressure toward undesirable conformity and its potentially destructive consequences. No doubt, Bryce's model of public opinion belongs to those liberal theories denounced by Habermas as reactionary, since they "reacted to the power of the idea of a critically debating public's self-determination . . . as soon as this public was subverted by the propertyless uneducated masses" ([1962] 1995, 136).

Later, when the level of literacy and general education increased accordingly, the rising significance of the masses in conceptualizations of public opinion is associated particularly with the mass (popular) press and propaganda. The relationship of the public to the masses takes the place of the former, dominant relationship to authority; it becomes an essential dimension of public opinion. The principle of tolerance of the majority (the uninformed masses) toward the minority (representative power) replaces the principle of the public controlling the actions of the authorities. Masses are increasingly regarded as "crowds," which—as Gustave Le Bon ([1895] 1930, 19) believes—"are only powerful for destruction," mentally inferior, and, essentially, "barbarian."[7] Le Bon's concern with the increased power of the crowd is followed by Gabriel Tarde's (1898) analytical distinction between the crowd and the public.

This shift in defining the contrasting side of the public is of crucial importance for the social-psychological and sociological understanding of public/ness that begins to gain prominence toward the end of the nineteenth century. The tendency to expand the concept of the public and to include the masses or the total citizenry has, without doubt, a democratic quality. An important consequence of sociologizing public opinion studies is the repudiation of predominantly unfavorable attitudes toward public opinion. The latter developed during the second half of the nineteenth century and reached their peak with Le Bon's study of the popular mind (1895), in which he treated even parliament as a crowd characterized by intellectual simplicity, irritability, suggestibility, and exaggeration of sentiments.

In a way, the twentieth century restores the tradition beginning with John Milton's assertion that "opinion in good men is but knowledge in the making," that is, a tradition of understanding opinion in general and public opinion in particular as attempts to recognize the truth and the common good. On the other hand—with this new perspective—the public loses its original rational-critical and political character. Whereas in pre–twentieth century normative theories, public opinion was conceived of as the result of the deliberation in the public as a social category—or in the public sphere as a public opinion context—twentieth-century empiricist schools of thought do not relate public opinion to any specific social entity or historical condition. From sociologizing public opinion to institutionalizing public opinion polling and advancing the spiral of silence model, the entire theoretical development in the twentieth century is characterized by controversies over the (non)democratic nature of public opinion.

In contrast to the critics of the democratic capacity of public opinion in the second half of the nineteenth century, French sociologist Gabriel Tarde developed in his book, *L'opinion et la foule* (Opinion and the Crowd, 1901), an alternative social-psychological paradigm based on his idea of imitation as "the elementary and universal social fact," together with invention and opposition. He recognizes the pressure to imitate—conversation being "the strongest agent of imitation"—and admits that "the need to agree with the public of which one is a part, to think and act in agreement with opinion, becomes all the more strong and irresistible as the public becomes more numerous, the opinion more imposing, and the need itself more often satisfied" ([1901] 1969, 318). Yet he also stresses the importance of internal (i.e., between different tendencies within a given person) and external oppositions to imitation which continuously bring about innovations. There are three principal forms of opposition: (1) war in the sphere of politics, (2) competition in economy, and (3) verbal discussion.

Tarde's conceptualization of public opinion is important as an alternative to the then dominant critique of majority rule. More specifically, his book incited Ferdinand Tönnies to start writing his book on public opinion. As he acknowledged in the preface to *Kritik der öffentlichen Meinung* (1922, v), a German publisher and writer, O. Hearing, made him aware of Tarde's book and suggested another book on that important topic. In other words, as Dewey's *The Public and Its Problems* (1927) appeared as a reaction to Lippmann's *Public Opinion* (1920), Tarde's book decisively stimulated Tönnies to pore over public opinion. Tönnies greatly appreciated Tarde's work, and although he widely disagreed with his "scientific assumptions," he largely incorporated Tarde's ideas into his own conceptualization of public opinion. For instance, Tarde's notions that "opinion is to the modern public what the soul is to the body," that the public is "a purely spiritual collectivity, a dispersion of individuals who are physically separated and whose cohesion is entirely mental," which started to develop "only after the first great development in the invention of printing," or that "a public and a church . . . are two aggregates ruled by different and irreconcilable principles"—clearly resemble subsequent Tönnies's theorization. That is also true of the relationship between belief and desire, two "internal dimensions of the soul" with their "reciprocal combinations," judgment and will, and "public opinion" and the "general will" as their generalized forms in society. This is not to say that Tönnies simply "imitated" Tarde's theory. He did not accept Tarde's strong inclination toward a sociological positivism that was strictly based on quantification, but he certainly utilized Tarde's psychological theorizing of conversation, discussion and opinion formation, and his view of public opinion as a social-psychological and cultural rather than merely political phenomenon.

Sociological conceptualizations that began to emerge in Germany and the United States in the early twentieth century brought about systematic studies of public opinion. During this time, critical interest in problems related to public/ness and public opinion became increasingly pronounced in the United States. American theorists soon gained preeminence not only by asking key questions but, even more so, by determining methods for finding their answers.

The newly emerging positivist paradigm treated public opinion as an organic social process and linked it to the social-psychological findings about group interaction—as "developing at the societal level out of communicative reaction to disagreement or ambiguity" (Price and Oshagan 1995, 195). Thus public opinion is progressively depoliticized, although early sociological theorizations continued to emphasize the political dimension of public opinion. The most prominent social theorists of public opinion of the time—Tönnies and Bauer in Germany and Dewey, Park, and Lippmann in the United States—explicitly refer to psychological research as a source (which is at least) as valuable as normative political theories of the eighteenth and nineteenth centuries. Blumer's definition of public opinion ([1946] 1966, 46–50)—representing the end of the classical (Chicago) sociological period and coinciding with the increasing use of public opinion polling—emphasizes the collective, interactive, and rational-discursive (but also manipulatable) characteristics of public opinion. He also stresses the competitiveness of groups that form the public as an "elementary and spontaneous collective grouping" that attempts to shape and set the opinions of relatively disinterested people. The public loses its strictly political character and its rigid reference to a national people. The issue that confronts the public is not constituted by its political characteristics but rather by the division of people "in their ideas as to how to meet the issue." The formation of the public only implies "the presence of a situation which cannot be met on the basis of a cultural rule but which must be met by a collective decision arrived at through the process of discussion."

During the first phase of sociologizing public opinion theories in the United States, a very important role is played by American pragmatism, represented by Charles Horton Cooley, William James, Charles S. Peirce, John Dewey, and George Herbert Mead. The tradition of American pragmatism and symbolic interactionism (Dewey, Mead, Blumer)—with its idea that society exists in communication—has left an important mark on theories of public opinion and communication. American pragmatism emerges from distinctive features of American society and history as an indigenous though heterogeneous tradition.

> It was a break with the absolutism which had dominated academic thought and an attempt to produce a philosophical context for social-scientific inquiries into the twentieth century with the aid of "biological imagination," and an emphasis on "human efforts," "collective action" and "meliorism." (Hardt 1992, 33)

Its most significant common denominator is "a future-oriented instrumentalism that tries to deploy thought as a weapon to enable more effective action" (West 1989, 5). Dewey emphasizes the practical and constructive role of reason in human action and defines pragmatism—distinct from the orientation of empiricism toward the past—as having an orientation toward the future "as an extension of historical empiricism but with this fundamental difference, that it does not insist upon antecedent phenomena but consequent phenomena; not upon the precedents but upon the possibilities of action. And this change in point of view is almost revolutionary in its consequences" (1931, 24).

Despite its indigenousness, the paradigm also owes much for its development to the European political-philosophical thought from which it descended; yet surprisingly—in contrast to earlier English contributions—it had almost no or an extremely limited impact on prevailing European theories of public opinion, including those of Tönnies and (later) Habermas. This is in sharp contrast to the empirical social-psychological tradition that developed in the United States and soon became the dominant theoretical force in most of Europe.

Pragmatism conceptualizes public opinion as primarily a communicative and interactive phenomenon. For instance, Dewey suggests that

> even if "society" were as much an organism as some writers have held, it would not on that account be society. Interactions, transactions, occur de facto and the results of interdependence follow. But participation in activities and sharing in results are additive concerns. They demand communication as a prerequisite. ([1927] 1991, 152)

Indeed, public opinion would remain a mere fiction without the substantial assumptions related to its communicative nature. "In politics communication makes possible public opinion, which, when organized, is democracy," according to Cooley (1909, 84). Public opinion presupposes freedom (and courage, as Kant would say) of expression, freedom of the press and thus human freedom in general; it also remains inseparably connected with the Enlightenment principle of publicity. Without the double determination of public opinion as the relationship and interaction (1) among citizens and (2) with the government, the concept of public opinion would lose its democratic import.

The pragmatists' understanding of the public and public opinion was based on the Rousseauian assumption "that each individual is himself equipped with the intelligence needed, under the operation of self-interest, to engage in political affairs" (Dewey [1927] 1991, 157). They vehemently refute the critique that democracy systematically produces mediocrity—as advanced by the theories of Tocqueville, Mill, and Le Bon in the nineteenth and Lippmann in the twentieth century. And they stress the importance of democratic forms of consultation and discussion (e.g., popular voting, majority rule), which serve to reveal societal needs. Dewey argues against Tocqueville's accusation that democracy generates mediocrity in its elected rulers and reflects the passions and foolish ideas of ordinary men, claiming that such a criticism in fact proves that democratic government is educational, which is not the case with other forms of government. Yet Park, in his early study of the public and the masses, observes an inherently contradictory character of the public and public opinion.

> What is usually called a public is a kind of group which stands for the most part at the same stage of awareness-development as the crowd. Thus, so-called public opinion is generally nothing more than a naive collective impulse which can be manipulated by catchwords. Modern journalism, which is supposed to instruct and direct public opinion by reporting and discussing events, usually turns out to be simply a mechanism for controlling collective attention. ([1904] 1972, 57)

Liberal theorists, who saw the principal danger of public opinion in its mass character and the subsequent potential for an intolerant majority, called for limitations on its excessive power. Pragmatists not only followed a different approach than liberals but they also kept a critical distance from the classical liberal theories of James Mill. They argued, instead, for the publication of sociological research in the daily press, for the translation of specialized knowledge into an accessible idiom, and for breaking down the ossified structure of social knowledge, whose backwardness "is marked in its division into independent and insulated branches of learning" (Dewey [1927] 1991, 171). Only with the wide application of science and scientific methods could a "democratically organized public" develop. Similarly to the early tradition of a classical liberal theory of public opinion that emerged from the (utilitarian) theory of freedom of the press, pragmatists linked their critical understanding of public opinion to a critique of a sensational press and the journalistic profession. Like their German contemporaries, Tönnies and Bauer, they emphasized the need for press reform and the complete independence of newspapers. They saw the press as the social sensorium that could potentially fill the great void of all hitherto existing social evolution. "The press for these thinkers was not paper, ink, words, and images; it was a set of social and imaginative relationships that could reconstruct, or further ruin, community life" (Peters 1989, 250). The pragmatists demanded not only freedom of the press and freedom of expression but, even more importantly, freedom of social inquiry and distribution of its findings.

Pragmatists, and particularly Dewey, greatly stressed the close link between the goals of social democratization and the development of knowledge in the process of transforming the Great Society to the Great Community. The latter, according to Dewey, is nothing less than "an organized articulate Public." The pragmatists' understanding of public opinion has much in common with Tönnies's ideas articulated in *Kritik der öffentlichen Meinung*. For example, his emphasis on the significance of science, in general, and the social sciences, in particular, the autonomy of the media and their educational function, and, most of all, the close link between the true public opinion and *Volksgemeinschaft*, which should be based—as a modern form of *Gemeinschaft* or socialism—on social reforms carried out in *Gesellschaft* (Tönnies 1922, 573).

Dewey assigned an important role in the transformative process to the dissemination of scientific research findings and, in particular, those of the social sciences. In his words,

> communication of the results of social inquiry is the same thing as the formation of public opinion. This marks one of the first ideas framed in the growth of political democracy as it will be one of the last to be fulfilled. For public opinion is judgment which is formed and entertained by those who constitute the public and is about public affairs. . . . Opinions and beliefs concerning the public presuppose effective and organized inquiry. ([1927] 1991, 177)

Yet pragmatism would later be the target of criticism—particularly harsh in the new social-psychological tradition—that public opinion had been unjustifiably reduced to its political control function, which was supposed to be exercised by specific institutions and mechanisms, and conceptualized as a sort of "systemic-conformist institution of the veto" (Schmidtchen 1959, 259).[8] But probably the sharpest critic—particularly of Dewey's unconditional confidence in public opinion and the idea of the "omnicompetent individual"—was Lippmann. He firmly believed that troubles of the press, popular government, and even industry have a common source, "the failure of self-governing people to transcend their casual experience and their prejudice, by inventing, creating, and organizing a machinery of knowledge" ([1922] 1965, 365). Since people are constantly and effectively exposed to vague, emotion-engaging symbols and stereotypes produced by the authorities and experts who generate public opinion and thus are unable to understand and decide highly complex social issues, it would only be reasonable, according to Lippmann, that the business of politics be left to the experts.

Contrary to the sociological tradition in the first half of the century from Park to Mills—which modernized the idea of citizen presence in an antique Greek square or Roman forum, or replaced it by defining the terms of an efficient collective action, especially on the basis of (parliamentary) representation—a German constitutional lawyer, Carl Schmitt, nostalgically defended a conservative version of "government by public opinion" ([1928] 1954). The latter is founded on the notion of people directly present in a certain space, which allows for a version of direct democracy similar to that expressed by Rousseau in his *Social Contract*. In a way, even Dewey, Schmitt's contemporary, excessively argued for the importance of direct communication and dialogue in a local community, claiming that "unless local communal life can be restored, the public cannot adequately resolve its most urgent problem, to find and identify itself" ([1927] 1954, 216). However, Dewey also emphasized the historical urge to surmount the borders of territorial states and political boundaries, whereas Schmitt's conceptualization was based on the notion of nation-state.

According to Schmitt, only when citizens gather in a shared space can they call to life the essence of public opinion—public acclamation; a mere tallying of votes and opinions of individuals cannot build public opinion by itself. Public opinion cannot arise through secret individual polling or aggregate opinions of isolated private persons. All of these recording methods may be expedient—and as such useful and valuable—yet they certainly do not constitute public opinion. For Schmitt, *public opinion is the modern art of acclamation*. There is no democracy and no state without public opinion, as there is no state without acclamation. Public opinion rises and exists "unorganized"; it would be deprived of its nature, and so would be the acclamation, if it became a sort of official function (Schmitt [1928] 195, 246).

In Schmitt's opinion, acclamation means that people can express their agreement or disagreement through exclamation (or they can keep quiet or murmur); to do so, however, requires physical presence. People produce the public by their very presence, and their specific activity in the public is acclamation, which is—according to Schmitt—linked to the constitutional right of assembly as a basis of democracy. Demonstrations, public celebrations, theater audiences, spectators at stadiums, and similar modern forms of assembly are modeled after antique forms; they do not represent organized forms but are potentially always political. Schmitt was primarily pointing to the process of "ignoring assembled people" in bourgeois democracies. He also emphasized the nondemocratic quality of secret voting used by "liberal individualism" to compensate for the fundamental assumption of any democracy—that the people cannot be represented because only what is absent can be represented, whereas the people always must be present, which was equated by Schmitt to mean "actually gathered people." However, Schmitt's different forms of people's gathering, supposed to constitute the basis of the public, are forms that Park saw as typical examples of the *crowd*.

By the halfway point in the twentieth century, American pragmatism had intellectually run out of steam, surrendering its dominant position in the study of public opinion to a new social-psychological paradigm. When Dewey published *The Public and Its Problems* in 1927, the book attracted much less attention than Lippmann's ideas, in both the United States and Europe. The expansion of polling in the 1930s and the establishment of *Public Opinion Quarterly* in 1937 actually marked the end of a fruitful theoretical era for pragmatism and the beginning of social-psychological approaches to public opinion. Nevertheless, the questions raised by pragmatism and the subsequent controversy between Lippmann and Dewey in the 1920s not only had a strong impact on the era but would also exert their influence in later years with the development of public opinion polling in the 1930s. Indeed they would leave a decisive mark on the intellectual history of debates regarding public opinion, the mass media, and democracy, even though the political and economic ascent of public opinion polling after World War II would push critical theories of public opinion into the background.

More recent notions, particularly commonly shared images of public opinion, are closely related to the development of polling. In his discussion of the nature of public opinion in *The American Commonwealth*, Bryce identified three stages in the evolution of public opinion. According to his scheme, in the (until then) most developed phase, the sovereign multitude expressed its will at certain intervals—in elections. However, according to Bryce, a fourth stage could be reached "if the will of the majority of the citizens were to become ascertainable at all times, and without the need of its passing through a body of representatives, possibly even without the need of voting machinery at all" ([1888] 1995). Bryce believed that this stage was utopian because "the machinery for weighing or measuring the popular will from week to week or month to month has not been, and is not likely to be, invented."

His prediction obviously proved wrong—the "machinery" was invented only a few decades later in the form of public opinion polls, almost in the very form predicted a few years earlier by Schmitt, who, in a cynical way and alluding to the American "voting machines," anticipated that someday, "without leaving his apartment, every man could continuously express his opinions on political questions through an apparatus, and all these opinions will be automatically recorded in the head office" ([1928] 1954, 245). He expressed what turned out to become very soon the mainstream conceptualization of public opinion. Since the mid-1930s, polls have also become functionally important in the political process in the United States and, after World War II, in all democratic societies.

During the latter 1920s, interest in questions of communication and media changed from theoretical considerations and social criticism—based upon the expectation of progressive thought—to practical concerns and specific problems within the scope of emerging research methodolo-

as a period during which the social sciences orchestrated at-
restrict social-problem and reform-oriented theory and research
and to develop disciplinary knowledge primarily with the help of empirical investigations. The social-psychological study of public opinion
was—particularly in its earliest period preceding World War II—predominantly directed toward empirical and quantitative opinion research. The
previously close relationship between public opinion, political democracy, and freedom of the press was replaced by a close empirical linkage
between public opinion polling, analysis of (particularly international)
propaganda, and the development of public relations. Public opinion was
largely reduced to a "multi-individual situation" (Allport 1937) or, according to Helmut Bauer's suggestion, to "the sum of all relevant individual opinions, as a cut through the peoples' opinions. It is thus nothing
but summing of equal or at least similar opinion expressions of citizens
inquired by ballot or opinion polls" (Bauer 1965, 121).

In everyday language public opinion is most often equated with simple
aggregation, "the summing-up of individual opinions," that is, with direct
"research objects" in public opinion polling. The result is a sort of "seriali-
zation of individuals," according to Jean-Paul Sartre (Beaud 1993, 134).
This notion of public opinion appears as a radical expansion of the opin-
ion-making function of society and thus seemingly "democratizes" public
opinion. One of the first prominent U.S. pollsters, George Gallup, believed
that polling ought to compensate for the growing limitations of a parliamentary democracy. At least during the early period of polling, summing
up individual opinions was supposed to help the voice of the people reach
the ears of authority. Such an understanding of public opinion was at odds
with the political-philosophical and early sociological traditions, which
had conceived of public opinion—in the words of Charles H. Cooley—as
"no mere aggregate of individual opinions, but a genuine social product, a
result of communication and reciprocal influence" (1909, 121). Indeed,
public opinion became an object of empirical research in the period following a commodification of politics and the "eclipse" of the public, as
Dewey suggested. It improved (rather than caused) the reliability and effi-
ciency of harmonizing mass consciousness (public opinion) with dominant opinions and interests. The role played by public opinion polling may
be compared to the role of "mature" mass media, which Dewey and Lippmann—followed by Mills and Habermas—described as failing to provide
the public with the kind of information and opinions that could provoke
discussion and connect people in a conversational community.

The notion of public opinion in empirical opinion research has ceased
to mean an existing unity. "Political opinion polls provide a certain reflection of 'public opinion' only if they have been preceded by a focused
public debate and a corresponding opinion-formation in a mobilized pub-

lic sphere" (Habermas [1992] 1997, 362). On that account one could speak of mass opinions (a collection of individual opinions) but definitely not of a unified public opinion. Not only is the true object of public opinion polling not public opinion, but it is not even aimed at opinion(s) as a form of holding for true; it only measures private attitudes.

With the reduction of public opinion to individual opinions and its consequent separation from the social context in which individuals interact, however, differences between the public and the masses (or the crowd) lose any meaning. The science of public opinion is interested in the final result (i.e., individual opinions) rather than in the actual social processes of generating public opinion. In addition, scholarly interest in scientific-methodological issues becomes the most important determinant of social research agendas in which "we have tended to overlook that there is a political content in what we call public opinion" (Berelson 1952, 313).

In contrast to Bernard Berelson, Herbert Blumer stresses that this tendency is much more than the result of an unintentional neglect and argues that

> the isolation of a generic object . . . is a goal rather than an initial point of departure—and that consequently the present inability to identify public opinion as a generic object is not damning to current public opinion polling. . . .
> However, what impresses me is the apparent absence of effort or sincere interest on the part of students of public opinion polling to move in the direction of identifying the object which they are supposedly seeking to study, to record, and to measure. . . . Their work is largely merely making application of their technique. (1948, 542)

Blumer also argues for a new research direction—symbolic interactionism—which emerged from the democratic tradition of the Chicago School and pragmatism—in particular the work of Robert Park and George Herbert Mead—and in opposition to Talcott Parson's functionalism and empiricism in social research. For Blumer, equating opinion polling with research on public opinion is a perfect example of the invalid dismissal of the interaction. The latter involves the direct reciprocally oriented social action between groups and individuals with varying amounts of influence and who, in their interaction, create and express public opinion (1948, 545). He perceived the public to be an essential component of the democratic process and, in keeping with the pragmatist tradition, considered empirical research of the nature and development of public opinion, for the most part, a method of stimulating interest and expressing opinions.

Yet methodological developments in the first half of the twentieth century, worshiped by social psychologists, also helped expel some normative illusions about public opinion. For example, normative-political theories largely ignore (as do early social-psychological approaches until the mid-1930s) differences between opinion and action, or issue and participation attitudes: individual opinions or attitudes are viewed as "more or less *decisive predispositions toward behavior*" (Lemert 1981, 30; emphasis added). Social-psychological research proves that there is no one-to-one correspondence between attitude and behavior. As Seemann (1993, 14) suggests, perhaps the most promising idea is to understand attitudes as mediators between an individual's social setting and situational circumstances and the range of potential behaviors. The idea that opinion expression as a form of behavior is also a function of the situation in which it is expressed belongs to the classic, nineteenth-century, normative-political theories, American pragmatists (notably Cooley and Mead), and to Tönnies. Social psychologists rediscovered it, and in the 1960s the idea was promoted, particularly by Erving Goffman and Milton Rokeach (Seeman 1993, 6), with the aim of making normative theories empirically testable. However, recognizing the importance of the situational component in opinion or attitude expression alone does not yet lead to significant methodological progress, although it resulted in some interesting approaches.

From American pragmatism onward, theorizing public opinion stressed its transformation under the influence of the mass media. The latter have been—in one way or another—the most important instruments of public opinion formation, expression, and manipulation since its first conceptualizations. Although the media have never been organized so that "virtually as many people express opinions as receive them"—which is the first condition for the public to exist, according to C. Wright Mills ([1956] 1968)—they never had been more powerful than after the rise of television. Mills was skeptical regarding the concept of the public as expressed in classical democratic theory and compared it to fairy tale images. Similarly, Habermas ([1962] 1995, 201) noted that a regression occurred in the development of the public sphere, so that the public was "refeudalized." The public was transformed into "the court before whose public prestige can be displayed—rather than in which public critical debate is carried on." The autonomy of public opinion and free public access to the means of communication—which are considered decisive by theorists of democratic public opinion—have become vulnerable and restricted even in democratic societies. In total contradiction to classical ideas of democratic pluralism, it became clear that the persuasive power of the media is even greater in pluralistic than in totalitarian societies. Indeed, relatively early on it was Lippmann who warned,

> The creation of consent is not a new art. It is a very old one which was supposed to have died out with the appearance of democracy. But it has not died out. It has, in fact, improved enormously in technic. . . . Persuasion has be-

come a self-conscious art and a regular organ of popular government. ([1922] 1960, 248)

Media power is at the core of the two most resounding—but mutually exclusive—contributions to the field after World War II in Germany: Habermas's "structural transformation of the public sphere" ([1962] 1995) and Elisabeth Noelle-Neumann's "spiral of silence" ([1974] 1980, 1993). The latter model represents one of the most outstanding crests in the social-psychological stream of thought. Noelle-Neumann revived the pre-Enlightenment dichotomy of *popular* versus *public* opinion—labeled as the difference between "social control" and "rationalist" functions of public opinion. She claimed that the power of public opinion can only be explained if public opinion is conceptualized in terms of "social control." In fact, Noelle-Neumann resumed and radically pacified and individualized postwar German and earlier American and British behavioral traditions (Splichal 1999). Curiously enough, she tried to relate her theory to Tönnies's theory of public opinion, although the latter is its radical *negation*. While her model certainly contributed to intensify endeavors to bridge the gap between theory and empirical research, its theoretical relevance remains rather insignificant.

Habermas's intellectual project initiated with his *Strukturwandel der Öffentlichkeit* is far more important. During his earliest period, Habermas understood the public as the bearer of public opinion, imbued with the function of a critic in relation to power. But he limited the validity of the term "public opinion" and the liberal model of the public *(Öffentlichkeit)* to their historically specific meanings in England and France at the end of the seventeenth and in the eighteenth century, respectively ([1962] 1995). Later, he defined the public as a "communication structure which is, through its base in a civil society, rooted in the life-world," and he concluded with examining its political functions in relation to "communicative power" and "deliberative politics" as an "alarm system" (Skerlep 1996, 379). According to Habermas, the contemporary notion of publicness, particularly in the sense of critical publicity, only provides some kind of comparative standard or radical democratic vision at the normative level, allowing for a critique of the deficiencies of existing (non)democratic institutions and relationships. Within the framework of a normative theory of democracy, the notion of a rational public opinion as a state-legal fiction points toward the unity of a "counterfactual entity" (Habermas 1992a, 440). Public opinion as "the rational opinion which emerges from the civil society and does not therefore mean the same as the opinion of particular groups of voters or the opinion of the electorate globally considered" remains a radical democratic vision without actually existing (or even being able to exist) in reality. In that sense it neither represents nor is an aggregate of individual opinions and therefore is impossible to operationalize it so as to coincide with the results of opinion polling.

The "postmodern" conceptualizations of public opinion (e.g., Thompson 1990; Peters 1995; Mayhew 1997) challenged Habermas's rational-discursive theory of public opinion, albeit from an entirely different perspective than Noelle-Neumann's empirical paradigm. Instead, they proceed from changes in the economy, politics, and culture brought on by the rise and massive use of new information and communication technologies to revolutionize earlier processes and conceptions of public opinion. In contrast to Habermas's theory, "postmodernists" emphasize the *representative* rather than the *surveillance* role of contemporary public opinion and the media, a role that is not necessarily opposed to enlightenment or rationality, although the importance of the latter is clearly declining. Also, the representative function is not understood in the Habermasian sense (i.e., as the manifestation of feudal "representative publicness"), which denotes public representation of power. Rather, mass media are considered autonomous power centers that organize meaning and identity and provide authoritative information for masses of people, structure their political preferences, and simplify the process of democratic power seeking activities previously earmarked largely for political parties, mainstream religion, the nuclear family, the workplace, and neighborhood, and social-class groupings.

Rational theories—and primarily Habermas's ideas—have been blamed for the historically incorrect neglect of dealing with the actual exclusion of large social groupings (e.g., women, workers) from the public. In addition, they supposedly did not realize that contemporary developments in communication technologies and publicity have changed communication and political processes so that the general accessibility and active participation of citizens in the formation and expression of public opinion have been invalidated even as normative ideals. These processes have been supposedly replaced by the "mediatization of politics" (Thompson 1990) and the "rhetoric of presentation" (Mayhew 1997). Thompson strongly argues against Habermas's refeudalization theory. He suggests that "the development of mass communication has created new opportunities for the production and diffusion of images and messages, opportunities which exist on a scale and are executed in a manner that precludes any serious comparison with the theatrical practices of feudal courts" (Thompson 1990, 115). New communication technologies, primarily television, increase the visibility of political leaders and limit their control of information flow, which moves audiences away from passive consumers. From a different perspective, Jean-François Lyotard (1979, 106) also argued against Habermas's earlier discursive conceptualization of the public, suggesting that there are no universally valid pragmatic language rules as a necessary condition for reaching consensus in a rational discourse; nor can consensus be the (only) purpose of dialogue.

In spite of the changed circumstances and new controversies, public opinion is still much more than a fiction, mystery, or blind alley—as Habermas, Lippmann, or Allport would say. According to Peters (1995), public opinion since its eighteenth-century origins always had a significant, symbolically constructed component and never existed apart from mediated representations, in the sense of Benedict Anderson's *imagined community*, whose most representative example is *the Nation*. "As long as political life is not centered on a single place where the people can assemble as a single body, the expression of the people's voice(s) will always be inseparable from various techniques of representation" (Peters 2000). Another reason for the assumed necessity of political representation is that most social "facts" (at the same time, socially produced facts) are not directly accessible to all citizens, except through "techniques of representation." Parliaments, media, and polls are the most distinctive institutionalized forms of such "techniques." Indeed, the function of representation and thus the representative nature of public opinion is inseparable from the phenomenon of public opinion.

A typical process in which imagined communities originate is the ceremony of "almost precisely simultaneous consumption (imagining) of the newspaper-as-fiction," which individuals perform in private but realize that the same "ceremony" is performed simultaneously by thousands of other anonymous, private persons (Anderson [1983] 1991, 35). One can see the roots of Anderson's idea in Tarde's and Tönnies's conceptions of "the large public" consisting of "spiritually connected" members. Tönnies understood the public as an essentially *political* and *moral* phenomenon, whereas Tarde's ideas were closer to postmodern, largely *depoliticized* conceptualizations. For Peters, public opinion is generated by some sort of symbolically formed "imagined public." Instead of direct interaction among individuals, symbolic representations of the social whole are circulated among them—primarily through the media—to help stimulate action as a social entity. The formation of a postmodern or, as Mayhew (1997) calls it, *New* public is much more affected by mass media, and television in particular, than by contiguous interactions among members of the public. Such an imagined public is nonetheless as real as any other imagined community in the sense that "in acting upon symbolic representations of 'the public' the public can come to exist as a real actor. . . . Fictions, if persuasive, become material, political reality" (Peters 1995, 18–19).

The idea that the media "replaced" interactions is neither new nor well grounded. Tarde argued that "if no one conversed, the newspapers would appear to no avail . . . because they would exercise no profour on any minds." In other words, "interaction" always existe stituent part and mover of public opinion, but its role varied with regard to other factors, and the media certainly modified it to great extent. Tarde believed that "public opinion has always existed whereas the public . . . is fairly recent" ([1901] 1969, 297)—resulting from the development of newspapers. The significance of the press was in its symbolic power—its ability to disseminate idea(l)s and persuade readers. According to Tarde, newspaper readers do not form a public because they read the same news, but only when they "are seized by the idea or the passion which provoked it" ([1901] 1969, 288). Such ideas are always produced by knowledgeable personalities (although the public is usually unaware of that) and spread by the media to be frequently reproduced or imitated among the people and thus gradually generalized. Before the rise of newspapers only thousands of individual and local opinions existed. Public opinion appeared when the press provided a link between local opinions and, at the same time, "suppressed the conditions which made possible the absolute power" of the king who alone was aware of local opinions and in a position to influence them. Newspapers "began by expressing opinion" and, as Tarde suggests, "ended up directing opinion almost as they wished" and becoming "omnipotent not only against tradition . . . but also against reason." Indeed Tarde stressed those characteristics in public opinion as a form of the "social mind" constantly fed and limited by two other rival forms, "Tradition" and "Reason," which are beyond any historical boundary and have universal validity or—as the postmodernists would argue—represent a kind of anthropological law.

Similarly to Tarde and Tönnies, postmodernists—however vague this notion is—believe that the classical political-philosophical pre-Revolutionary concept of an enlightened public opinion conceals the anthropological regularities of opining as a procedure of sharing differences and individual interests, which speaks in favor of a sociological approach. The public sphere is conceptually pluralized by taking into account the plurality of subjects (individuals, groups, institutions, associations) publicly expressing opinions. Indeed, the idea of a sociological aggregate, "the public," did not exist until the eighteenth century, when the bourgeoisie replaced the "body" as a model of a political society with the communicative practices of critical debate and print. Public opinion as "common opinion" or "mentality"—as proposed by Beaud and Kaufmann (1999)—emphasizes the actual historical development and the social context of opinion formation, in contrast to normative conceptualizations in which public opinion is grounded in a disinterested communicative action. Baker's distinction between rumors, extra-institutional, and institutional channels of opinion production and expression—the basis for Beaud's and Kaufmann's criticism of the idealization of a single public (the public) of reasoned men—is reminiscent of Tönnies's differentiation between published opinion, public opinion, and the public's opinion. The three historical social practices, typical of different social classes, are competing but also coexisting. Thus there is no justification for being obsessed with "king's gestures and the words of educated" while neglecting the "changes of world-view of ordinary people."

The problem of representation relates to *externalization*. Park and Blumer already emphasized that public opinion is not a unanimous opinion of everyone in the public sphere but an opinion that is external to every individual and viewed as objective. As Park ([1904] 1972) suggests, precisely because public opinion is a product of individual critical attitudes, it is expressed differently by different individuals. The process of externalization is not specific to public opinion. Similarly, an artistic performance is expected to enable each spectator to watch his "own" performance, or to create it uniquely in his mind, thus making the "objective" performance "external" to the author's scenario. The idea of "externality" can also be found in empirical opinion research in the "paradox of pluralistic ignorance." Many studies document that *perceptions* of an agreement or a majority opinion actually affect individual behavior, rather than agreement itself or the actual majority opinion; the two do not necessarily correlate. One can imagine an extreme case in which no one agrees with an opinion but everyone believes that all (but he or she) do agree and behaves as if everyone actually agreed.

Nevertheless, the changes experienced in the late twentieth century do not justify in themselves the final rejection of the idea of an enlightened public opinion. As Dewey argued in his controversy with Lippmann, "Until secrecy, prejudice, bias, misrepresentation, and propaganda as well as sheer ignorance are replaced by inquiry and publicity, we have no way of telling how apt for judgment of social policies the existing intelligence of the masses may be" ([1927] 1991, 209). Danilo Zolo (1992), for example, argues similarly with Habermas that the neoclassical doctrine of democracy remains without satisfactory explanatory power and calls for an entire reconstruction of democratic theory. Such a theory must take into account the fundamental changes in (the relationship between) the private and public spheres, as well as changes in the legitimization processes of mass democracies, as suggested by Habermas, but in a much more critical way. There are several reasons for such a critical reassessment. (1) The asymmetrical, noninteractive nature of mass-political communication is developed to such a degree that the idea of an "electronic democracy" has definitely become utopian. (2) By its further dispersion—and primarily as a consequence of the "narcotizing dysfunction" of the mass media—the public sphere transformed itself into "a reflexive area, a timeless meta-dimension in which the 'real' public passively assists, as if in a sort of permanent television broadcast carried out in real time, in the exploits of an 'electronic' public" (1992, 166). These two tendencies are taking on world-wide proportions and are bringing about "a second structural transformation of the public sphere" that is global and more radical than the one analyzed by Habermas in the 1960s, because, according to Zolo

> the sovereignty of the political consumer—i. e., the autonomy, rationality and moral responsibility of the citizen called upon to pass sovereign judgment on the competition between parties—can now hardly amount to more than empty verbiage in the context of the massive spectacularization of teledemocracy to which pluralistic competition between the parties . . . is being reduced. (1992, 170)

This presentation of milestones in Western public opinion theories permits a consideration of ideas that significantly influenced Tönnies's *Kritik der öffentlichen Meinung*, which will be the subject of the next chapter. But it appears equally clear that the theories of public opinion developed after World War II, including German ones, totally and—as we shall argue—unjustly ignored his contributions.

## NOTES

1. Binkley (1928, 389) reports: "On the question when is opinion public, the round table was unable to come to a definite conclusion. The main points of disagreement were as follows: 1. whether there is and must of necessity be a single public opinion, or whether there may be a number of public opinions upon a given question; 2. whether opinion is public because of the subject matter to which it relates or the kind of persons who hold it; 3. what part of the public must concur in an opinion to make it public; 4. and must there be acquiescence by those who do not concur."

2. Ginsberg's and Zaller's preference for "mass opinion" is not founded on the public opinion–mass opinion dichotomy, in which mass opinion is a negation of public opinion, as suggested, for example, by Tönnies (1922, 77–87) and later by Schmidtchen (1959).

3. Modern public opinion is, as a matter of fact, conceptualized as a phenomenon closely linked with the *nation-state*. This "matter of fact" was particularly emphasized by public opinion polling in which respondents are randomly selected from the population of citizens. Thus citizens represent a sort of "natural" population despite the fact that modern states at best exist no more than a few centuries (but often only a few decades or even a few years). Regardless of whether such equalization is justified or not, there obviously exist other forms of expression and representation of (public) opinion that are less (or not at all) institutionalized and involve relatively small numbers of individuals and/or groups.

4. Nevertheless, Rousseau clearly states that (1) the role of the censor is not to judge "the opinion of the people" but only to express it and (2) though censorship can contribute to the preservation of, for example, customs, it cannot change them.

5. And if these groups already exist, it is necessary (1) to ensure that there are as many of them as possible and (2) to prevent inequality among them.

6. In contrast to Tocqueville, whose *Democracy in America* he assesses—despite his general admiration of the work—rather critically ("it is not democracy in America he described, but democracy illustrated from America"), Bryce notes that "the tyranny of the majority does not strike one as a serious evil in the America of today" ([1887] 1995, 1567). Nevertheless, Bryce lists the tyranny of the majority, "which enslaves not only the legislatures, but individual thought and speech, checking literary progress, preventing the emergence of great men," among seven "clouds on the horizon" ([1887] 1995, 1569).

7. "It cannot absolutely be said that crowds do not reason and are not to be influenced by reasoning. However, the arguments they employ and those which are capable of influencing them are, from a logical point of view, of such an inferior kind that it is only by way of analogy that they can be described as reasoning" (Le Bon [1895] 1930, 73). Yet Le Bon's contempt for crowds also extends to the "crowds in parliamentary assemblies," which are characterized by "intellectual simplicity, irritability, suggestibility, the exaggeration of the sentiments and the preponderating influence of a few leaders" (Le Bon [1895] 1930, 315).

8. Criticism also came from the opposite side. Carl Schmitt ([1928] 1954, 249), for example, criticizes Tönnies's concept of public opinion, which was in many respects similar to the concept of the American pragmatists. Schmitt acknowledges that it was "the most important sociological research on the subject" but criticizes it for not fully advancing the *political* character of public opinion.

## REFERENCES

Allport, Floyd H. 1937. "Toward a Science of Public Opinion." *Public Opinion Quarterly* 1, no. 1: 7–23.

Anderson, Benedict. [1983] 1991. *Imagined Communities: Reflections on the Origins and Spread of Nationalism.* London: Verso.

Baker, K. M. 1990. "Public Opinion as Political Invention." In *Inventing the French Revolution: Essays on French Political Culture in the Eighteenth Century,* 167–199. Cambridge: Cambridge University Press.

Bauer, Helmut. 1965. *Die Presse und die öffentliche Meinung.* Munich: Günter Olzog.

Bauer, Wilhelm. [1933] 1963. "Public Opinion." In *Encyclopedia of the Social Sciences,* edited by E. R. A. Seligman, 669–674. New York: Macmillan.

Beaud, Paul. 1993. Common Knowledge. *Reseaux, French Journal of Communication* 1, no. 1: 119–128.

Beaud, Paul and Laurence Kaufmann. 1999. "Policing Opinions: Elites, Science, and Popular Opinion." *Javnost-The Public* 6, no. 1: 5–27.

Beniger, James R. 1987. "Toward an Old New Paradigm: The Half-Century Flirtation with Mass Society." *Public Opinion Quarterly* 51, no. 4, pt. 2: S46–S66.

Berelson, Bernard. 1952. "Democratic Theory and Public Opinion." *Public Opinion Quarterly,* Fall, 313–330.

Binkley, Robert C. 1928. "The Concept of Public Opinion in the Social Sciences." *Social Forces* 6: 389–396.

Blumer, Herbert. 1948. "Public Opinion and Public Opinion Polling." *American Sociological Review* 13: 542–554.

Blumer, Herbert. [1946] 1966. "The Mass, the Public, and Public Opinion." In *Reader in Public Opinion and Mass Communication*, edited by B. Berelson and M. Janowitz, 43–50. New York: Free Press.

Bourdieu, Pierre. [1972] 1979. "Public Opinion Does Not Exist." In *Communication and Class Struggle*. Vol. 1, *Capitalism, Imperialism*, edited by A. Mattelart and S. Siegelaub, 124–130. New York: International General.

Burke, Edmund. [1769] 1967. "The British Empire and American Revolution." In *Selected Writings and Speeches of Edmund Burke on Reform, Revolution, and War*, edited by Ross J. S. Hoffman and Paul Levack, 46–112. New York: Knopf.

Bryce, James. [1888] 1995. *The American Commonwealth*. 2 vols. Indianapolis: Liberty Fund.

Childs, Harwood L. 1939. "By Public Opinion I Mean . . ." *Public Opinion Quarterly*, April, 327–336.

Childs, Harwood L. 1965. *Public Opinion: Nature, Formation, and Role*. Princeton, N.J.: van Nostrand.

Converse, Philip E. 1987. "Changing Conceptions of Public Opinion in the Political Process." *Public Opinion Quarterly* 51, no. 4, pt. 2: S12–S24.

Cooley, Charles Horton. 1909. *Social Organization: A Study of the Larger Mind*. New York: Scribner's.

Dewey, John. 1931. *Philosophy and Civilization*. New York: Minton & Balch.

Dewey, John. [1927] 1991. *The Public and Its Problems*. Athens: Swallow.

Ginsberg, Benjamin. 1986. *The Captive Public: How Mass Opinion Promotes State Power*. New York: Basic.

Glynn, Carroll J., and Jack M. McLeod. 1984. "Public Opinion du Jour: An Examination of the Spiral of Silence." *Public Opinion Quarterly* 48, no. 4: 731–740.

Habermas, Jürgen. [1965] 1980. *Teorija i praksa* (Theory and Practice). Beograd: Kultura.

Habermas, Jürgen. 1992. "Further Reflections on the Public Sphere." In *Habermas and the Public Sphere*, edited by C. Calhoun, 421–461. Cambridge: MIT Press.

Habermas, Jürgen. [1962] 1995. *The Structural Transformation of the Public Sphere: An Inquiry into a Category of Bourgeois Society*. Cambridge: MIT Press.

Hardt, Hanno. 1992. *Critical Communication Studies: Communication, History, and Theory in America*. London: Routledge.

Hegel, Georg Wilhelm Friedrich. [1821] 1971. *Philosophy of Right*. Translated with notes by T. M. Knox. London: Oxford University Press.

Kant, Immanuel. [1795] 1983. "To Perpetual Peace." In *Immanuel Kant: Perpetual Peace and Other Essays*, 107–144. Cambridge, Mass.: Hackett.

Keane, John. 1992. *Mediji in demokracija*. Ljubljana: Znanstveno in publicisticno sredisce.

Key, V. O., Jr. [1961] 1967. *Public Opinion and American Democracy*. New York: Knopf.

Le Bon, Gustave. [1895] 1930. *The Crowd: A Study of the Popular Mind*. London: Ernest Benn.

Lemert, James B. 1981. *Does Mass Communication Change Public Opinion after All? A New Approach to Effects Analysis*. Chicago: Nelson–Hall.

Lippmann, Walter. 1925. *The Phantom Public*. New York: Harcourt, Brace.

Lippmann, Walter. [1922] 1960. *Public Opinion*. New York: Macmillan.

Luhmann, Niklas. 1971. "Systemtheoretische Argumentation." *Theorie der Gesellschaft oder Sozialtechnologie*, by J. Habermas and N. Luhmann, 291–405. Frankfurt: Suhrkamp.

Luhmann, Niklas. 1994. An Interview with David Sciulli. *Theory, Culture, and Society* 11, no. 2: 37–69.

MacKinnon, William A. [1828] 1971. *On the Rise, Progress, and Present State of Public Opinion, in Great Britain, and Other Parts of the World*. Shannon: Irish University Press.

Marx, Karl. [1842] 1969. "Die Verhandlungen des 6. rheinischen Landtags." In *Pressefreiheit und Zensur*, by K. Marx and F. Engels, 44–99. Frankfurt: Europäische Verlagsanstalt.

Marx, Karl. [1843] 1974. "Zur Kritik der Hegelschen Rechtsphilosophie." In *Marx–Engels Werke*, 1:202–336. Berlin: Dietz.

Mayhew, Leon H. 1997. *The New Public: Professional Communication and the Means of Social Influence*. Cambridge: Cambridge University Press.

Mead, Margaret. [1937] 1965. "Public Opinion Mechanisms among Primitive Peoples." *Public Opinion and Propaganda*, edited by Daniel Katz, D. Cartwright, S. Eldersveld, and Alfred McClung Lee, 87–94. New York: Holt, Rinehart, and Winston.

Mill, John Stuart. [1859] 1985. *On Liberty*. London: Penguin.

Mills, C. Wright. [1956] 1968. *The Power Elite*. London: Oxford University Press.

Negt, Oskar. 1980. "Mass Media: Tools of Domination or Instruments of Emancipation? Aspects of the Frankfurt School's Communications Analysis." In *The Myths of Information: Technology and Postindustrial Culture*, edited by K. Woodward, 65–87. London: Routledge & Kegan Paul.

Newcomb, Theodore M. 1950. *Social Psychology*. New York: Dryden.

Noelle–Neumann, Elisabeth. 1974. "The Spiral of Silence: A Theory of Public Opinion." *Journal of Communication* 24, no. 2: 43–51.

Noelle–Neumann, Elisabeth. [1980] 1993. *The Spiral of Silence: Public Opinion–Our Social Skin*. Chicago: University of Chicago Press.

Park, Robert E. [1904] 1972. *The Crowd and the Public*. Edited by H. Elsner Jr. Chicago: University of Chicago Press.

Peters, John D. 1989. "Democracy and American Mass Communication Theory: Dewey, Lippmann, Lazarsfeld." *Communication* 11, no. 3: 199–220.

Peters, John D. 1995. "Historical Tensions in the Concept of Public Opinion." *Public Opinion and the Communication of Consent*, edited by T. L. Glasser and C. T. Salmon, 3–32. New York: Guilford.

Peters, John D. 2000. "Realism in Social Representation and the Fate of the Public." In *Vox Populi, Vox Dei?* edited by S. Splichal. Creskill, N.H.: Hampton.

Price, Vincent, and Hayg Oshagan. 1995. "Social–Psychological Perspectives on Public Opinion." *Public Opinion and the Communication of Consent*, edited by T. L. Glasser and C. T. Salmon, 177–216. New York: Guilford.

Rousseau, Jean Jacques. [1762] 1947. *The Social Contract*. Translated by C. Frankel. New York: Hafner.

Schacht, Richard L. 1972. "Hegel on Freedom." In *Hegel: A Collection of Critical Essays*, edited by A. MacIntyre, 289–328. Garden City, N.Y.: Anchor.

Schmidtchen, Gerhard. 1959. *Die befragte Nation: Über den Einfluss der Meinungsforschung auf die Politik.* Freiburg: Romabach.

Schmitt, Carl. [1928] 1954. *Verfassungslehre.* Berlin: Duncker & Humblot.

Seeman, Melvin. 1993. "A Historical Perspective on Attitude Research." In *New Directions in Attitude Measurement,* edited by D. Krebs and P. Schmidt, 3–20. Berlin: de Gruyter.

Skerlep, Andrej. 1996. "Analiza druzbenega konteksta komunikacijskih procesov." Ph.D. diss., University of Ljubljana.

Splichal, Slavko. 1981. *Mnozicno komuniciranje med svobodo in odtujitvijo.* Maribor: Obzorja.

Splichal, Slavko. 1999. *Public Opinion: Developments and Controversies in the Twentieth Century.* Lanham, Md.: Rowman & Littlefield.

Tarde, Gabriel. [1901] 1969. "The Public and the Crowd." In *Gabriel Tarde on Communication and Social Influence,* edited by T. N. Clark, 277–318. Chicago: University of Chicago Press.

Tocqueville, Alexis de. [1840] [1912] 1995. *Democracy in America.* http://darwin.clas.virginia.edu/(tsawyer/DETOC. Originally scanned and corrected by T. G. Roche at the University of Virginia (June 15, 1995) from *Democracy in America,* by Alexis de Tocqueville. Translated by H. Reeve. New York: Appleton, 1912.

Thompson, John B. 1990. *Ideology and Modern Culture.* Stanford: Stanford University Press.

Tönnies, Ferdinand. 1922. *Kritik der öffentlichen Meinung.* Berlin: Julius Springer.

Vreg, France. 1980. *Javno mnenje in samoupravna demokracija.* Maribor: Obzorja.

West, Cornel. 1989. *The American Evasion of Philosophy: A Genealogy of Pragmatism.* Madison: University of Wisconsin Press.

Wilson, Francis Graham. 1962. *A Theory of Public Opinion.* Chicago: Regnery.

Zaller, John R. 1992. *The Nature and Origins of Mass Opinion.* Cambridge: Cambridge University Press.

Zolo, Danilo. 1992. *Democracy and Complexity: A Realist Approach.* University Park: Pennsylvania State University Press.

# Tönnies, Public Opinion, and the Public Sphere

*Slavko Splichal and Hanno Hardt*

The dominant social-theoretical approaches of the twentieth century (and particularly empirical research) either are indifferent to earlier normative-theoretical conceptualizations of the public and public opinion or explicitly renounce them. But there are some significant departures from the mainstream, which are represented by American pragmatism and, most notably, Ferdinand Tönnies (1855–1936), the German sociologist whose theory has been unjustly ignored in twentieth-century discussions of public opinion.

Tönnies's neglected, if not largely forgotten, theoretical writings result from the most comprehensive effort to conceptualize public opinion as a form of *social will*. His critical theory of public opinion represents one of the most significant classical social-theoretical contributions to the field, and a unique effort to make public opinion an integral part of a complex and refined general social theory. Consequently, it gives preference to the complex processes in culture and society over their partial, institutionalized forms in politics and the state. Yet, like many other social theories originating at the beginning of the twentieth century, Tönnies's theory is much less influential at present than more practical-minded and empirical approaches developed after the 1930s.

Tönnies's attempts at theorizing public opinion had been preceded by the writings of political economists like Albert Schäffle, Karl Knies, and Karl Bücher, and French social psychologists like Gabriele Tarde and Gustave Le Bon. Their writings emerge in the context of social and economic developments in Europe, including urbanization and industrialization, and produced a climate of intellectual curiosity and practical concerns

over issues of public opinion formation and its social and political consequences. Among Tönnies's German colleagues Schäffle addressed the
press as a "large, connected system of cells which collect and reproduce
ideas, and as such is an 'organ of public opinion.'"[1] Knies extolled the effects of the telegraph as an instrument of unifying the social system and
acknowledged the interdependence of the cultural and economic spheres
of society.[2] Bücher dealt with the rise of the modern press as an organ of
public opinion capable of carrying public opinion as well as influencing
it.[3] Elsewhere he had characterized the press as

> a marvel of economic division of labour, capitalistic organization, and me-
> chanical technique; it is an instrument of intellectual and economic inter-
> course, in which the potencies of all other instruments of commerce—the
> railway, the post, the telegraph, and the telephone—are united as a focus.[4]

In his own dynamic conceptualization of public opinion as a form of
complex social will, Tönnies recognized the mutual influence of public
opinion and other forms of social will. Opinion of the public, with "the
public" as its subject, differs from other forms of social will in that the
unanimous will is a result of knowledge; it is formed by rational judgment and "competes" in *Gesellschaft* with two other forms of the complex
social will—convention and legislation. In his comprehensive book *Kritik
der öffentlichen Meinung*, Tönnies (1922) pursues theoretical and historical
analyses of differences between published opinion, public opinion, and
opinion of the public; he theorizes the relationship between religion and
public opinion, analyzes three "aggregate states" of the opinion of the
public (gaseous, fluid, and solid), and conceptualizes the role of the press
as a means of expressing and influencing public opinion. Although the
press and parliament may be considered the most important "organs of
opinion of the public," they are, as Tönnies critically observed, more often
than not instruments of influencing and then expressing public opinion.

Unlike earlier theories that focused on phenomena that occur in specific
*social places*, Tönnies conceptualized public opinion beyond the boundaries of physical settings: he saw "the public" as a form of imagined intellectual grouping, whose members share similar ideas and opinions
without interacting directly. In his examination of public opinion he elaborated on a variety of essential elements in the communication process.
He recognized the importance not only of signs but also of audience characteristics, message construction, communicator functions, and roles of
the mass media (e.g., books and newspapers). Public opinion is not en-
forced by physical or external means (e.g., money) but through ideas that
lead to enlightenment; as such it has, as moral judgment, normative validity. Tönnies's theory offers grounds for a critique of institutional
arrangements (which dominated at that time but still exist today) and for

emancipatory actions, particularly in the sphere of the press. On the one hand, his theory is an attempt to integrate ideas of rationality, interactivity, and morality of public opinion, postulated by normative-philosophical and early psychological approaches to public opinion; on the other, it is in sharp contrast to a social-psychological tradition that has developed since the 1930s and has completely abandoned the idea of a *specific group* or collectivity in (by) which public opinion is formed and expressed. The *rationality* of (public) opinion formation was disavowed already by his contemporary, Walter Lippmann. In addition, both social-psychological approaches and the post-Tönniesian sociological tradition reject the idea that public opinion contains a *moral* dimension on which to base its validity for the collectivity; instead, the influence of public opinion has been related to primary psychological mechanisms (e.g., the individual's fear of social isolation) or to the numerical majority, as in conceptualizations of public opinion as statistical aggregations of individual opinions.

While Tönnies acknowledged the importance of pressures to conform in the process of generating public opinion (making public opinion similar to religion), he vigorously defended the importance of independent reasoning as the basis of the opinion of the public. His theory of public opinion gives a clear preference to culture over politics, and society over state. Tönnies understood opinion of the public as a "common way of thought, the corporate spirit of any group or association, in so far as its opinion formation is built upon reasoning and knowledge, rather than on unproved impressions, beliefs, or authority" (1922, 78). In this sense, opinion of the public may be considered a "rationalized" form of religion. However, his holistic theory also emphasized the unity of will and emotions that are expressed in reason, and the foundation of reason in human life processes: the rationality of opinion always implies the volitional and affective dimensions of opinion formation.

## A BIOGRAPHICAL NOTE

Tönnies showed a lifelong interest in the study of social and political problems; he was equally committed to securing the place of sociology in the university setting. His major and still distinguished contribution was his work in theoretical sociology, which began with the publication of *Gemeinschaft und Gesellschaft* in 1887. However, his subsequent fundamental work on public opinion, *Kritik der öffentlichen Meinung* (Critique of Public Opinion), published in 1922, has been curiously subjected to a "conspiracy of silence."

Tönnies was born in Oldenswort, Schleswig, Germany, in 1855, and he studied at the universities of Jena, Leipzig, Bonn, Berlin, and Tübingen between 1871 and 1877. He acquired an extensive background in philosophy, history, ancient languages, and archeology before he concentrated his studies in the social sciences. His *Habilitationsschrift* (professorial dissertation) in 1881 qualified him for a university-level teaching position. However, because of his liberal and materialist-rationalist views, the Prussian minister of education did not grant him a professorship until 1911, when he joined the faculty at the University of Kiel, Germany. He resigned five years later. At that time he had already published several works, including *Gemeinschaft und Gesellschaft* (1887), *Hobbes Leben und Lehre* (1896) and *Die Sitte* (1909). After his resignation, Tönnies devoted his time completely to his studies and to writing for scholarly and popular journals. *Kritik der öffentlichen Meinung* was published one year after he had returned to a teaching position at Kiel, in 1922. The completion of his third major work, *Einführung in die Soziologie*, fell into this period. It appeared in 1931, two years before he was forced to resign from his duties as a result of Hitler's rise to power. At that time he also relinquished his position as the first president of the *Deutsche Gesellschaft für Soziologie*, the German sociological association he had founded together with a number of colleagues, among them Georg Simmel, Max Weber, and Werner Sombart.

His philosophical studies had led Tönnies to the writings of Thomas Hobbes, Herbert Spencer, and August Comte. He had become interested in the organismic theories of both Spencer and Schäffle, which stimulated his curiosity about the biological sciences; he also took a great interest in philosophy of law, particularly as represented by Rudolph V. Jhering and Sir Henry Maine. Also, Hobbes's writings on law and government and Karl Marx's *Das Kapital* (1867) became major influences on his scholarly thought. Accepting the secularized concept of natural law and recognizing the importance of economic aspects of social life, Tönnies formulated his own approach to the study of society. He concluded from his study of the meaning of natural law that "what is social emanates from human willing, from the intention to relate to each other, a together-willing (*Zusammenwollen*), as it were; and I set myself the task of penetrating to the essence of this willing" ([1932] 1971, 4).[5] Although Tönnies accepted the basic ideas of historical materialism, he proposed a sociological rather than an economic explanation of society because economics—in his way of thinking—could not be identified with the well-being of individuals or community.

His studies of contemporary problems (e.g., crime, suicide, strikes) serve as examples of utilizing empirical sociology for understanding social conditions and providing a basis for critical judgment and correction of social ills. Also, his empirical studies reflect his continuing interest in his social and political environment and his engagement as a concerned social scientist who hoped to bring new insights to the task of improving social conditions in Germany. Given this commitment, Tönnies supported the Weimar

Republic and joined the Social Democratic Party in the wake of Hitler's rise to power as a demonstration of his own position, his political ideas, and, perhaps, as an example for others to step forward and become recognized opponents of the regime. Political activities—which he had avoided previously to protect his scholarly work—now surfaced on many occasions and reveal the intensity of his reaction to the rise of Nazism in Germany. For instance, in a letter to a Kiel newspaper, Tönnies suggests that

> Adolf Hitler talks foolishly . . . [and] knows nothing about the nature and causes of this catastrophe of the capitalist economic system. In his ignorance he blames the German working class and the party which represents the rights and interests of the German workers. The NSDAP is a party that *promises everything to everybody* in such a way that what has been promised to one contradicts promises given to others; it is a party which substitutes *deliberate disregard of truth,* massive errors and blind emotions for rational thought. *In short, it is a party to which a thinking person, particularly a politically thinking person, cannot commit himself.* ([1932] 1971, 286–287)

Because of his resistance to Nazism, Tönnies lost his position and also his pension. Ironically, after World War II his work was condemned on the ground that it substantiated national-socialist ideology—an "interpretation" similar to that blaming Marx's social theory for Stalinism.

Tönnies embarked on investigating public opinion in his first, best-known work, *Gemeinschaft und Gesellschaft* ([1887] 1991, 202–204, 214), and proceeded to develop his findings into a coherent theory in an extensive treatise, *Kritik der öffentlichen Meinung* (hereafter *Critique*). Published in 1922, it undoubtedly remains one of the most coherent analyses of public opinion ever written, yet it is practically absent from contemporary academic and nonacademic discourse on public opinion. A few fragmentary references and only six more thorough presentations of his ideas on public opinion exist. Following D. Koigen's (1925) review of *Critique* in *Ethos* (a German journal), Paul A. Palmer (1938) briefly introduced the work to the English-speaking world after Tönnies's death in 1936. Later treatments appeared in Wilson's *Theories of Public Opinion* (1962), Gillian Lindt-Gollin and Albert E. Gollin's contribution to a Tönnies reader edited by Werner J. Cahnman (1973), Hanno Hardt's *Social Theories of the Press—Early German and American Perspectives* (1979), and Slavko Splichal's *Public Opinion: Developments and Controversies in the Twentieth Century* (1999). Tönnies's ideas are clearly present in general discussions of public opinion only in the works of William Albig (1939, 1956), John Keane (1982, 1984), and Horst Pöttker (1993), who provide a comparative analysis of Tönnies's and Noelle-Neumann's conceptualizations of public opinion. None of thirty-five contributions to recent, representative publications— *Public Opinion and the Communication of Consent* (edited by Glasser and

Salmon 1995) or *Öffentlichkeit, öffentliche Meinung, soziale Bewegungen* (edited by Neidhardt 1994)—discusses Tönnies's theory of public opinion or at least offers an explicit citation. In addition, examinations of Tönnies's sociological theory tend to completely overlook his theory of public opinion (e.g., Merz-Benz 1995; Rudolph 1995).

There are several plausible reasons why Tönnies's epochal work did not resonate in the academic community. With the rise of Nazism, the human sciences in Germany faced the hardship shared by other enemies of the Third Reich. German *Zeitungswissenschaft* (science of the press) as an academic approach to journalism faded away and—together with other disciplines—surrendered its leadership in research to academic institutions in the United States, the new home of many exiled European researchers. Also, the affirmation of empirical research in the United States during the 1920s brought about a radical turn in the humanities. Until that time European empirical sociology and the humanities, in general, understood "empirical research" most of all as dealing with historical facts, while American empiricism introduced an empirical world of observation and data collection. American communication and public opinion research advanced most rapidly during and after World War II, when continental social studies began to advance distinctly under the influence of earlier U.S. developments.

In addition, Tönnies's theory of public opinion was significantly different from any American mainstream approach at that time, and in a sharp contrast to the post-Tönniesian behavioral tradition, which completely abandoned the idea that public opinion would be formed and expressed by a specific reference group or collectivity and that it would be *rational* and *moral* by its very nature. It was seen as "typically German," as Wilson (1962, 111) maintained, because it primarily addressed the "traditional, religious, and cultural circumstances" under which public opinion is formed, rather than the ways and the means with which public opinion effectively influences representative government. The latter is characteristic of the dominant modern Anglo-Saxon tradition, one that Wilson also adopted. Yet the theory that Tönnies brought to full development represents the continuation of a tradition originally endorsed not only in Germany. In fact, prior to sociologizing public opinion research in the twentieth century, most European theorists related public opinion to religion and the bourgeois class. For instance, William MacKinnon's book on public opinion, published in 1828 in London—although largely forgotten—actually laid the foundation to a European "cultural" tradition.

Also, since Tönnies lectured only briefly at the university, he was without students who could have further developed his theoretical thought. His articles published before the appearance of *Critique* (1922) suggest a sustained and systematic interest in public opinion, but they were scat-

In his discussion of the concept and theory of public opinion, Tönnies traces the idea of public opinion from individual to collective expressions, differentiating, finally, among six forms of collective will under the aspects of *Gemeinschaft* (community) and *Gesellschaft* (society). His theory posits two basic kinds of human relations that are subjectively grounded and—being a product of human nature—expressed in diverse forms of social structure (see table 1). He insists that *Gemeinschaft* and *Gesellschaft* are fundamental concepts that help define types of human existence:

> The meaning of these concepts is that all relations among people as well as the derived relations of social corporations with individuals and with each other, even the relations between men and their gods, which like social entities are products of their imagination—all these complexes of positive relations which constitute a bond among men—(*vinculum*) have a twofold origin: either man's organic will or his rational will. ([1925] 1971, 132)

The distinction between *Gemeinschaft* and *Gesellschaft* is essential for Tönnies's understanding of public opinion.[12] Community is a traditional and inarticulate form of social organization based on personal relationships, customs, and faith. The concept of society signifies an urban and industrial (i.e., a rational social) organization, in large cities and states, based on nonpersonal relations, special interests, conventions, law, and public opinion, respectively. In many ways this understanding is a reminder of the concept of *civil society*. Unlike community, which is based on similari-

Table 1   Forms of Social Will

| *Community* | *Society* |
|---|---|
| Elementary forms | Elementary forms |
| (A) understanding | (D) contract |
| (Verständnis) | (Vertrag) |
| (B) tradition | (E) norm |
| (Brauch) | (Satzung) |
| (C) faith | (F) doctrine |
| (Glaube) | (Lehre) |
| | |
| Complex Forms | Complex Forms |
| (AA) Concord | (DD) Convention |
| (Eintracht) | (Konvention) |
| (BB) Custom | (EE) Legislation |
| (Sitte) | (Gesetzgebung) |
| (CC) Religion | (FF) Public Opinion |
| (RELIGION) | (Die Öffentliche Meinung) |

*Source*: Tönnies (1922, 219).

ties among groups and individuals in terms of beliefs and actions, society is concerned with economic ("convention"), political ("legislation"), and moral ("public opinion") relationships among diverse groups. Society is also characterized by the central position of the middle class.

Despite the fact that *Gemeinschaft* and *Gesellschaft* are defined as normal concepts, they are obviously related to social, economic, and technological developments in late nineteenth-century Germany. The process of industrialization began considerably later in Germany than in Britain or France, but in the period between the mid-1800s and the beginning of World War I, the industrial and service sectors increased to 45 percent and 32 percent of the GNP, respectively, and to 38 and 27 percent of the active population. The size of the population almost doubled and reached 67 million during the same period before the war. Industrialization was accompanied by urbanization, so that on the eve of World War I 35 percent of the population lived in towns with more than 20,000 inhabitants, up from 12 percent in 1871. By the beginning of the twentieth century, illiteracy was practically nonexistent in Germany. These developments represented the material foundation of Tönnies's conceptualization of the transformation of the social structure from *Gemeinschaft* to *Gesellschaft*.

More specifically, in the realm of technology the transportation system, particularly railway traffic, also rapidly developed during the same time, largely due to substantial subsidies by the German state. Furthermore, the rise of telegraph and telephone communication in the late 1800s stimulated the rise of the press. The number of magazine titles tripled between 1875 and 1913, while the number of newspapers and their circulation doubled during the same period. There were over 6,600 magazines and over 4,000 newspapers with a total circulation of 16.3 million copies in 1913. By the end of the war, the number of magazines and newspapers decreased to 2,200 and 3,200, respectively, but the size of the total newspaper circulation increased to a remarkable 27 million! Again, Tönnies specifically referred to communication and transportation technologies as factors substantially contributing to the development of both *Gesellschaft* in general and public opinion, as its specific manifestation in terms of the social will, in particular. The rapid growth of the press sector (Tönnies's book on public opinion was published only one year before the first radio broadcast in Germany) was based on its commercialization and the expansion of advertising, which stimulated Tönnies to discuss its unfavorable "side effects" and the need for radical press reforms. Freedom of the press was constitutionally guaranteed in Germany as late as 1919, but even then it was considerably limited in practice. During the late 1800s, censoring and even banning newspapers were common practices (e.g., as a result of the Socialist Act of 1878, 42 socialist dailies were banned). Even in the Weimar Republic, the laws enacted to protect the republic actually limited press freedom.[13]

For Tönnies, community and society are ideal types that never exist in their pure forms; rather, various forms of communal and societal organizations may appear, in different degrees, simultaneously within the same social structure. Tönnies stresses the universal and "pure" theoretical character of "community" and "society" beyond the historical; at the same time, however, they may be applied to any concrete and historically determined form of life. It should not be overlooked (as several Tönnies interpreters have done) that *Gesellschaft* does not represent the last stage of development, neither in its pure theoretical nor in its historical-practical sense. The fact that the features of community are slowly disappearing while the attributes of society are prevailing does not mean that historical development is inclined toward *Gesellschaft*. Instead, Tönnies sees the future stage of development in a "people's" or "new" community, which he calls *Volksgemeinschaft* or *neue Gemeinschaft*, as a synthesizing stage of historical development. He never discussed *Volksgemeinschaft* as thoroughly as the first two categories because it does not represent an ideal type or, rather, because it does not have a normative meaning. *Gemeinschaft* is for Tönnies not just a specific historical structure from which *Gesellschaft* develops but also a model of future transformations of the latter. In fact, people's community is a synonym for socialism.[14] Constituted as reality and moral necessity (or as a matter of consciousness) for the first time during World War I, its nucleus is in a "healthy family life, the hearth of real morality that even the best of public education can only complete and refine, but it cannot replace it" (Tönnies 1922, 573). The opinion of the public can greatly contribute to the rise of a people's community as long as it emanates from this core and is empowered to link various worldviews and different parties and direct them toward mass social reforms. Thus in the future the opinion of the public could become a "social conscience" (*soziales Gewissen*), as religion had been in the past[15]; according to Tönnies, its likelihood depends primarily on the development of science—an idea found, for instance, in Dewey's work on the public.

There are some who reproach Tönnies for having favored the idea of community, since he (disproportionately) stressed the negative aspects of society, especially in his *Gemeinschaft und Gesellschaft* (Freund 1978, 154). This is partially true, considering his expectations of how *Volksgemeinschaft* would develop as community/society of the future, representing *Gemeinschaft* on a higher level of development (while also representing its negation, since *Gesellschaft* is a negation of *Gemeinschaft*). However, such blame cannot be sustained for his *Critique*. Despite its title—which represents a critique of an imprecise use of "public opinion" and calls for a more precise definition of its meaning—the complete work is dedicated to society. In it the opinion of the public is fully established and keeps its essential function, even in the *Volksgemeinschaft*.

Differences between *Gemeinschaft* and *Gesellschaft* correspond to differences between organic and rational wills: people create either community grounded in organic will or society founded on rational will. Tönnies understood *Gemeinschaft* as based on organic or essential will *(Wesenwille)*, with its roots in feelings, habits, and beliefs, and *Gesellschaft* as built upon rational or arbitrary will *(Kürwille)* as resulting from artificial, deliberate, or conscious acts in which means and ends are clearly separated, in a way similar to Max Weber's *zweckrationales Handeln*. With this description, he not only tried to depict the full range of human existence but also attempted to offer a new way of understanding the origin and growth of Western society. Together, organic and rational wills represent the totality of human nature expressed in social relations; their relationship equals the relationship between believing and opining. "Just as there is no water that is hydrogen, and another that is oxygen, there is no one will that is organic will, and another that is rational; rather, all the wills consist of, and are linked by, the organic and rational will" (Tönnies 1922, 18). Rational will is always based on organic will, and organic will is always expressed through rational will. Since neither exists in "pure form" in the experiential world, any differentiation between two "ideal types" is possible exclusively as abstraction or on the level of pure ideas. The prevailing form of will determines the pattern of human relations.

Tönnies conceives of social relationships as "willed" relationships, that is, wanted, planned, and maintained purposively by interrelated human beings, and influenced by the wills of others not directly involved in transactions. The latter idea is similar to Dewey's concept of "the public" denoting a specific entity formed by those "indirectly and seriously affected" by consequences of transactions in which they are not involved (Dewey [1927] 1991). Tönnies's understanding of "will" is based on psychological conceptualizations of his time but is also related to earlier philosophical conceptualizations of will by Rousseau and Hegel. Like Rousseau's "general will" or Hegel's "substantial will," Tönnies's forms of social will are normative constructs that cannot be equated with any of their empirical manifestations.

Human will (or consciousness) is conceptualized as the cause for or tendency toward action; it is characteristically symbolized by human freedom. Tönnies sees the difference between animal and human groupings principally in human volition and reasoning, in contrast to instincts characteristic of animal life. According to his own definition (in Loomis and McKinney 1996, 275 n. 19), individual human will is "every existing combination of ideas (thoughts and feelings) which, working independently, acts in such a way as to facilitate and hasten, or hinder and check, other (similar) combinations of ideas (makes them probable or improbable)."

Social will originates from members of a collectivity; it is common to them and binds them together and thus also determines their individual wills.

Will is closely connected to thinking *(Denken)* as "the most difficult, complicated, and important psychical activity" (Tönnies 1922, 4) of human beings. While the will is metaphysically understood as "the psychical equivalent of the human body," in which sentiments and mental moods are manifested, thinking—with "cognition" as its general function—exhibits the rational capabilities of the intellect. Organic will determines thinking (i.e., the will includes thinking), whereas the opposite is true for rational will: consciousness is liberated so that it is thinking that determines the will (i.e., thinking includes the will).

Social will is articulated as communal or societal will according to (1) its relation to social behavior and social activity; (2) within this framework, according to its relation to specific actions and to the dissolution of primarily common activities and a unified organized collectivity; and (3) how it is revealed in thought and in the recognition of reality, that is, in beliefs or in the ways individual opinions are formed (Tönnies 1922, 56). Although forms of societal will represent a negation of the communal will, they also emerge from it. Each complex form of the will has also a "forerunner" in a simpler form and a specific relationship with similar forms, as, for example, faith in tradition and understanding.

Organic will is characterized by the transrational elements in human nature, the rational will by the priority of reason. In organic will the stress is on the traditional, the emotional, and the absolute. Its opposite, the rational will, emphasizes instrumentalism and distinctions between goals and means. Since the forms of rational will are nothing but "rationalized" or "reflected" forms of organic will, the former always somehow depend on the latter. In community, forms of common will spring mainly from common emotions, but they derive from common thoughts in society. Moving from organic to rational forms of will represents a process of "fortifying" and formalizing; it becomes prominent, at least in simple forms of the social will, with the development of writing (Tönnies 1922, 220).

Both in community and society, the *elementary* forms of social will represent—most of all—nonbinding private decisions for the entire community or society or agreement between individuals and subgroups (not throughout community or society). However, *complex* forms of social will are an "expression of a collective will," but at the same time they have their basis in individual will. The basic difference between elementary and complex forms of social will resides in the degree of mandatory subjection: the collective will may achieve a high degree of agreement among members of a collectivity and enforce it among dissenters. Complex forms of societal will are derived and in fact "made" to correspond to the forms of individual rational will, while communal forms "spring up" and correspond to the forms of individual organic will as "experientially given will." Each form of complex social will governs one of the three types of norms: (1) order, (2) law, and (3) morality. Public opinion is the form of social will that sanctions norms of morality, similar to religion; law is created either by legislation or by customs, whereas convention and concord represent the most universal norm—order.

Tönnies exemplifies the contrast between organic will and rational will by introducing the difference between two forms of property. He suggests that

> the property of an organic will is so deeply attached to the essence of a person, with his/her soul, that parting with it necessarily creates a feeling of discomfort. The property of a rational will, to the contrary, causes happiness only in as much as it has the desirable result as an unconditionally desired consequence: this means that happiness effaces and often even compensates for the discomfort that is present also here. (1926, 19–20)

With the organic will's property *(Wesenwilleneigentum)*, subject and object typically become coupled and linked; moreover, the subject assimilates the object and gets attached to it because he or she created it, so that there is no clear separation of means and ends of human actions. Typical examples include relations with animals, plants, and other people, as well as with parts of productive property, such as with the house as a home or with a garden. In contrast, the rational will's property *(Kürwilleneigentum)*, brought about by the "commercial civilization," is considered an "expense." It is often nothing but a means for the people to reach a desired end. This contrast is also expressed in the changed relations between the individual and the social: in a community "the general is *prius*, and the specific and the private is *posterius*." In society it is the reverse: the specific comes before the general (Tönnies 1926, 23).

Tönnies's theory represents a realization that the unity of will and emotions is expressed in reason and that reason is grounded in human life processes; therefore, physical and cultural domains cannot be separated. Like American pragmatists, particularly Dewey, he strives for an integral academic inquiry into human beings and nature, separated by increasingly scientistic specialization and fragmentation. On a macro-sociological level, Tönnies advocates evolution and materialist or "realist" interpretations of history: reason, thought, and institutions are products of material, historical processes and interests, but these processes and interests in return (dialectically) also influence the former (Cahnman 1973, 7). His holistic and humanist views about human beings and society are present also in his efforts to link rationalism and empiricism, two traditions that had hitherto been considered exclusive.

# PUBLIC OPINION IN THE MATRIX OF FORMS OF COMPLEX SOCIAL WILL

Tönnies devotes half of the first book of *Critique* to a systematic, comparative, etymological analysis of terms like "opinion," "thought," "determination," "will," and "faith." He provides proof for an interconnectedness between ideas, thoughts, convictions, opinions, beliefs, and will. His understanding of "opinion" basically derives from Immanuel Kant's conceptualization of three levels of *Fürwahrhalten* ("holding for true") in his *Critique of Pure Reason* ([1781] 1952), which are determined by the subjective and objective validity of judgments.

Beginning with his understanding of opinion as will, Tönnies outlines the opinion of the public as a form of social will in society (*gesellschaftlicher Wille*), that is, as a form of *rational* will[16]—more precisely, one of its "higher" or more complex forms—in contrast to forms of *communal* will, which are exemplified by religion. In terms of its relations to other forms of social will (see table 1), opinion of the public is determined in three ways (1922, 77–78, 229–230):

1. In its relation to *religion* as a corresponding/opposite form of communal will; thus as reflexive will in general is a rationalized form of organic will, opinion of the public is a rationalized form of religion. Both represent a form of spiritual and moral collective will, and opinion of the public performs in society the role religion does in traditional "community."
2. In its relation to *doctrine* as a corresponding elementary form of societal will: just as faith and religion form a totality, so do opinion of the public and doctrine.
3. In its relation (difference) to the subjects of other *forms of the complex societal will—law and convention*: the subject of convention is society, the subject of legislation is the state, the subject of opinion of the public is "the public" or "public," with the "republic of the learned" (*Gelehrtenrepublik*) at its core.

Tönnies (1916, 1928) presents the primary tasks of a critical theory of public opinion by explicitly relying on his predecessors, among them Christoph Martin Wieland and Christian Garve. These tasks involve determining five differences to help establish a more precise meaning of his "opinion of the public" (Tönnies 1922, vi):

1. The difference between *public opinion* and *opinion of the public*, partly taken from Emil Löbl,[17] is that the former is a conglomerate of various controversial views, desires, and intentions, whereas the latter is a unified force, an expression of a common will.

2. The difference between opinion of the public in its *historical and po-litically decisive sense* (opinion of the public has an immense influence on politics) and *ephemeral* public opinions, which are, although uni-fied, present throughout social life in their limited, partly local, and partly nonpolitical sense.
3. The difference between three basic aggregate states of opinion of the public with which Tönnies wishes to specify the properties of opin-ion of the public on an applied level.
4. The difference between public opinion (and opinion of the public), popular beliefs *(Volksstimmung)*, and popular feelings *(Volksgefühle)*.
5. The difference between opinion of the public and religion, which are similar and related as well as incompatible and divergent.

In his *Critique*, Tönnies discusses extensively the relationship and dif-ferences between public opinion (as an experiential phenomenon) and opinion of the public (as a pure theoretical concept), and between opinion of the public and religion. He proceeds to apply his results to the charac-teristics of the three aggregate states of opinion of the public in different areas, without following up, however, with a systematic discussion of the difference between public opinion and public beliefs—although his intro-duction suggests that this difference is crucial for understanding opinion of the public. Thus the difference between public opinion (or opinion of the public) and popular beliefs remains only a formal-theoretical one. Whereas public opinion is typical for the modern *Gesellschaft,* as well as for the societies or communities of the future (e.g., *Volksgemeinschaft*), pub-lic beliefs belong to the traditional *Gemeinschaft.* According to the charac-teristics Tönnies associates with the gaseous opinion of the public, it is practically (i.e., empirically) impossible to determine a clear, meaningful difference between a "gaseous" (i.e., least solid) opinion of the public and public beliefs.

Since his early works, Tönnies has considered public opinion enlight-ened and rational, that is, a form of social will based on rational will and agreement between individual (private) and public opinions. Indeed, only for this reason can reasonable individuals act according to their opin-ions (Gollin and Gollin 1973, 185). Opinion of the public is a form of a complex collective will associated with the ethical and aesthetic dimen-sions of collective life, whereas convention is associated mainly with the general and the economic, and the legislature with political life. In other words, according to Tönnies (1922, 228), convention is, in fact, a regula-tion *(Vorschrift;* i.e., a recommendation or directive) and legislation is an order *(Befehl;* i.e., a mandate or an interdiction), whereas an opinion of the public is a judgment *(Urteil)*. In *Gemeinschaft und Gesellschaft,* Tönnies—for the first time—defines public opinion as a form of social will and power

major differences between the two in *the degree* of seriousness and rigor to enforce and sanction their rules in the fields of order, legality, and morals. In all these fields, and particularly in the field of morals, religion is more rigorous than public opinion. Among all forms of complex will, opinion of the public is, by Tönnies's definition, the form of social will *least jeopardized by silencing dissenting voices*. "The new, the modern, the enlightened way of thinking" is, according to Tönnies, the strongest in the public and has an irresistible power. In Park's ([1904] 1972) terms, opinion of the public refers to those forms of interaction that *are beyond* primitive forms of reciprocity observed in the animal herd or suggestive *imitation* of surrounding social forms exemplified by the crowd.[23]

Complete agreement is unattainable, although it exists as a permanent tendency to overcome the fluid state of the opinion of the public. However, Tönnies nowhere explicitly defines the opinion of the public, which corroborates his principled belief that it is possible to reveal forms of appearance of public opinion and (mis)perceptions of it (this is why his book is entitled *critique* of public opinion), whereas it is very difficult to determine what really is the opinion of the public (1923, 72).[24] Nevertheless, we can conclude from his articles (1916; 1928) that, for all practical purposes, he entirely accepts Garve's rationalistic definition, formulated at the end of the eighteenth century. Garve wrote:

> Public opinion . . . is an agreement of many, or of a majority of citizens of a state about judgments that would be acceptable for every individual according to his own reasoning or experiences. . . . Opinion of the public cannot be equated with a habit *(Herkommen)*, a custom *(Gewohnheit)*, or with effects of learning. It cannot mean an agreement which could change a legislature, or an established religion into a way of thinking for a nation, or create an influence of a strong and articulate individual in a political party. Where only one man thinks and evaluates, while the rest blindly believe him or merely repeat his words, . . . there is no public opinion—which always presupposes that a man who treasures it, follows his own nature and impressions in his judgments. (in Tönnies 1916, 415)

Opinion of the public does not represent a discursive agreement but a naturally initiated feeling of agreement, when the opinions of many people essentially influence and support those actions and changes in state and Church that are compatible with these opinions (Tönnies 1928, 45). According to Tönnies, only Garve's words "of many, or of a majority" need to be replaced in his definition by "all citizens" to obtain "a concept that will probably never correspond to reality but would, for this very reason, become a strictly scientific, mathematical concept, or, as Kant says, an idea" (1916, 415). In this sense, opinion of the public is closely linked to education, that is, to enlightenment *(Aufklärung)*, according to Garve. Tönnies emphasizes that the prospects of participating in the formation of an opinion of the public depend on an individual's education. Consequently, the development of public education is definitely important for the progress of an opinion of the public, yet only a minority holds the degree of "higher education" needed for an independent formation of opinion, unprejudiced judgments, and critical evaluation independent of external pressures. Complete independence in forming opinion, as postulated by Garve, is still an ideal rarely reached in reality.

Opinion of the public differs from other forms of social will by the *manner in which the unanimous will is formed*. The unanimous common will can be a result of knowledge and formed by a rational *decision* reached by an individual or accepted by many people. The latter case expresses a desire for action and expectations for everyone to conform to a common aspiration. A new collective body, a unit capable of "making decisions" (e.g., a society, a club, a cooperative, a political party, a committee), may be established by such a decision. Accepted and agreed upon in advance by an individual or a group (e.g., according to a group's bylaws and by majority vote), such a decision becomes a decree and, therefore, binding for the membership. The topic of such a decree may even be the *expression of opinion*, which concerns *aspirations*, but not the *formation of opinion*, which concerns *reasoning*.

The decision-making process (i.e., "a regular form of the rational unification of the will") may serve as a model for every *rational* (in contrast to organic) common will and its effects. Whereas the decision presupposes a unit, or an artificial subject that represents all members of a group, common will can be expressed by an *agreement* between two or more individuals (or groups) that does not imply any artificial "subject." Rather, it is shaped by the sum of numerous individual wills. The object of an agreement (i.e., what individuals want) can even be objectified in the sense that the agreement is positioned outside of individuals and separated from them without implying that these individuals are objectified as subjects of this aspiration. Thus the agreement can be transmitted or published in a completely independent, objectified form.[25]

Yet there is a third alternative of how to obtain a unified will: unanimity is reached by expressing the same opinion at a meeting or by discovering a generally acceptable opinion "formula." For Tönnies, achieving agreement makes sense on a spiritual and moral level—typically in an *opinion of the public*. In contrast to unanimity achieved by decision, no majority convinced of the correctness of the opinion is needed here. However, a basic tendency to form a unanimous will by contract always exists regarding the fundamental social order.

# PUBLIC OPINION IN PURE THEORY
# AND APPLIED RESEARCH

Tönnies's theory of opinion of the public is a critique of public opinion; it is primarily directed against popular views about public opinion and toward establishing a scientific understanding. In popular conceptions, public opinion is understood simply as publicly expressed opinions.

> The published opinion, in this sense, has only this essential property that it is uttered or communicated, and this, moreover, "in general" ways. Namely, it is transmitted to any listener or reader, in contrast to 1. an opinion that is by nature internal and personal (intimate), and also in contrast to 2. an opinion that is confidentially conveyed to specific, known persons. If an opinion, thus transmitted, becomes an opinion and a judgment of the many, even a majority, i.e.,—if its weight is judged by the weight of a majority of a meeting—if it is a judgment of a unity, a circle, or a unity that is united into a community or society, then we could call it a public opinion. (1922, 129–130)

Any closed or open circle can generate an indefinite or arbitrary public opinion if its members assign a specific weight to it (e.g., opinions of a town, profession, stratum, or class) and act accordingly. As soon as members of different strata gain freedom of speech and press, a host of various, even opposing and publicly expressed, opinions rise directly from this collective freedom of expression. In this sense, public opinion is far from unanimous (1922, 129). The public nature of public opinion is by itself limitless; however, many practical barriers obstruct the "reception" of published opinion, according to Tönnies, for example, (1) the language of communication; (2) the relevant political area, where the issue of opinion is meaningful; (3) the level of education among readers and listeners; (4) the strength of the spiritual and moral "voice"; (5) the opinion circles of recipients; (6) the "external" communication media, especially the size of the public in the periodical press (1922, 135–136).

Nevertheless, Tönnies's concept of public opinion does not correspond to what pollsters want to measure in public opinion polls (cf. Gollin and Gollin 1973, 196). Indeed, Tönnies treats public opinion as a collective and public phenomenon, even when it appears as a "phenomenological unity" of different and opposing opinions that can easily find their way into the press, and not merely as an aggregate of (quasi-private) opinions that can be expressed by various means. Media in which public opinion can be expressed may be "natural" or "artificial," that is, they are only used or misused. Besides the press, Tönnies also lists formations of associations, meetings, demonstrations, festivities, or social occasions where followers gather—the most frequently used medium of public opinion (where misuse is represented, e.g., by deceptive news). The latter means of expressing public opinion most prominently expose their common features, namely, praising people and respectfully addressing and inviting them to join in or to express their opinion. The newspaper is the most common and general medium of expression for all of them. Tendency among newspapers to praise is mostly concealed, yet it is present. Newspapers also flatter their readers and tempt them to accept agreement, not as a matter of course but validated by reasoning.

These means of expression do not serve only opinions. They also promote objectives for which publishing opinions is useful, for example, gaining the opinion of the public, promoting an idea or a person, or influencing a change to a favorable opinion. According to Tönnies, it would be wrong, however, to think it possible to grasp the opinion of the public by what we hear or see in streets and town squares or read in newspapers (1923, 73–78). In fact,

> opinion of the public is expressed as a social and political power by approving or disapproving political events, demanding certain hearings from its own government, requiring the elimination of specific weaknesses, pressing for particular reforms and legislative action; in short, by "taking a point of view" about certain questions like interested bystanders would judge them. (1923, 77)

Newspapers, in particular, may both express an opinion of the public or influence public opinion. Equalizing popular public opinion and opinion of the public, however, is misleading because it suggests that newspapers are organs of opinion of the public or even identical with it (Tönnies 1923, 78). In reality, newspapers are, most of all, organs of political parties, and only metropolitan newspapers (which are read by an educated public) yield information about the opinion of the public. Specifically, even if these newspapers are not organs of opinion of the public, they can influence such an opinion at least indirectly.[26] If anything, only parliament may be called an "organ of opinion of the public," but even this is not always justified (1923, 77). Whereas insignificant places may have their public opinion, opinion of the public necessarily has a national, or even international and transnational, character. Public opinion appears in various ways, but most strongly and efficiently in newspapers, where it can actually proceed into an opinion of the public. This occurs, for example, when the most reasonable and substantiated opinions about public affairs are published in the most important newspaper, although rarely if published in only one of them. We can talk about opinion of the public when the same opinion is rephrased by several newspapers and approached beyond partisan bias. This "flow of public opinion" causes even those newspapers that do not support a particular opinion to yield in order to escape the opposition of their readers; journalists present an opinion without personally agreeing with it. Nevertheless, newspapers, in general, do not form the opinion of the public but merely report on a "case" without *intending* to form an opinion of the public. The opinion flow, or "the wind of opinion of the public," blows from opinion leaders with a very explicit, volitional component (together with rational and affective ones).

Tönnies's genuine interest is not in *inarticulate* public opinion; only *opinion of the public*, where a (large) audience, the *public*, acts to form and express an opinion, is worthy of scientific inquiry and theoretical analysis. Opinion of the public substantially differs from public opinion precisely in its subject: whereas public opinion does not have any specifically defined subject,

> the subject of opinion of the public is an essential, politically united public, in particular, which has agreed to opine and judge in a particular way and which, therefore, belongs naturally to the public and public life. . . . Opinion of the public is essentially a will expressed in and through a judgment— as a cohesive act—and, therefore, is a conscious and expressed form of the will in the manner of a judicial order or judgment by any other decision-making body. It is an agreed-upon decision—the expression of the will of a totality which is not gathered as an audience or subject of opinion of the public, except in spirit, and which is typically too large to be represented as a gathering. (1922, 131-132)

Thus both concepts of public opinion are characterized by a publicly communicated opinion and deal with public, mostly political affairs. A general and colloquial connotation of "public opinion" is not totally irrelevant for a scientific conception, but it is still more important to understand what has been established by the "called upon thinkers" (1916, 420 n.).[27] Tönnies determines the fundamental difference between colloquial understanding (= public opinion) and scientific conception (= opinion of the public) by the subject; the subjects of an opinion of the public are spiritually connected, or "gathered," individuals, who debate and reach a conclusion, whereas public opinion has no evident subject. Opinion of the public is a "general, common opinion of the people or the public, in other words, a form of social will that is in all its forms expressed as a unified will, as a will of one person."

Tönnies approaches the public as "the judge that judges as opinion of the public": the judge must know the truth and judge morally (1923, 83, 92). The ethical opinion of the public has to be able to recognize the truth first and then judge each case by the basic law. In the experiential world, this idea can only serve as an ideal: "It would be foolish to expect an enactment of such an idea, or to suppose that it could be accomplished by rules or preachers," Tönnies admits. At the same time, he emphasizes that "setting up a goal is always necessary in order to give rational endeavor its direction. If we do not have an ideal of the opinion of the public in our hearts, every effort to *bring up* a true opinion of the public will be in vain" (1923, 97).

A large part of his *Critique* is devoted to a detailed historical description and a (less elaborate) theoretical analysis of the public(s). Opinion of the public in recent centuries presupposes a "large public," which is the only "proper public" (*"das" Publikum*); it is composed of a "limitless mass of people who, in spite of being dispersed and infinitely diverse, may think and judge similarly" (1922, 84).[28] The large public is never spatially joined, that is, gathered in one place at a certain time, as publics in the past (e.g., a theater audience) were. A large public functions within many "circles" where it becomes audible. A public is formed by certain kinds of events (e.g., in politics, science, arts, or connected with "outstanding personalities") by people who are capable and willing to pass judgments about such events and have "appropriate skills and education—members of an educated world," according to Tönnies (1922, 84). A "large public" constitutes unity, spatially limited by a nation (at least in his time), determined by attention to a public issue, and therefore temporarily and internally divided according to the firmness of a formed opinion. Thus publics (in plural) are never really public, as was noticed much later by Arato and Cohen (1996, 136), while adopting Habermas's idea of the "mass public." Tönnies speaks of publics only at an applied-historical level, where publics act solely as carriers of public opinion (and not of an opinion of the public). It was characteristic of (narrow) publics to limit access, and they neither attracted public attention nor had a "real public" (1922, 103).

In Tönnies's times a public was nearly exclusively a "newspaper reading public." The interest of a large public was directed mainly at economic problems with frequently related political questions; therefore, the large public was a political public. Inside the political opinion of a public (or the opinion of a political public), one or more particular public opinions may exist, related to specific questions and issues, according to Tönnies (1923, 82 n.). Public opinion is, as a rule, divided, while an articulated opinion of the public is characterized by its attempt at unity. A large political public is typically less international than particular publics and more conditioned by the specifics of a state. Nevertheless, world events have their international publics. The most important differences between publics are linked to general, and specifically political, education. A public is "an idea of undetermined width and lasting" and usually unconfined by space or time (1922, 85). The more a public as a carrier of social consciousness is a politically or at least spiritually and morally connected unity, "the more its shared view and conviction approach the opinion of the public" (1922, 231).

Only a public consisting of spatially dispersed yet intellectually connected individuals distinguished by their education, political impartiality, and support for general public interest can act as subject in the formation of an opinion of the public. It is characterized by political nonpartisanship, absence of special interests, and support of the "general good." Most of all, a genuine opinion of the public, as a prudent "worldview," remains above political parties and their goals. Lippmann (1925, 112) wrote almost identically about the properties of public opinion later, stressing that the "true public" has to purge itself of groups with particular interests who become mistaken for it.[29] Dewey ([1927] 1991, 121) also agreed that "American party politics seem at times to be a device for preventing issues which may excite popular feeling and involve bitter controversies from being put up to the American people" and stressed "the pre-eminence of the claims of the organized public" (organized "in and through those officers who act on behalf of its interests") over other interests ([1927] 1991, 27–28). Because of these assumptions, the development of a large public and an opinion of the public are predominantly associated with urbanization; compared to rural environments, large cities most noticeably represent the difference between *Gesellschaft* and *Gemeinschaft*.

Similarly, Dewey claims that a public cannot develop in primary groups (i.e., in "community life"). He suggested ([1927] 1991, 27) that the basic definition of the public proceeds from the distinction between the results of interpersonal transactions, which the people involved can control by themselves, and indirect consequences, to which people not directly involved are exposed. Accordingly, the public as a specific grouping differing from different forms of community life is formed by "those indirectly and seriously affected for good or for evil" by consequences of transactions in which they are not involved—to such a degree that a systematic regulation of the consequences is believed necessary (Dewey [1927] 1991, 35, 16). The interest in implementing a restricting or an encouraging regulation is assumed by public officials; the regulation cannot be implemented by the primary groupings themselves. Dewey concluded, in contrast to Tönnies, that a public must also be formally organized as a political state to be actually effective. In a state or a public, the government consists of officers and agencies with special duties and authorizations who act on behalf of the interests of the public. Although Tönnies's theory also proceeds from the difference between community life and a (large) public, he sees the problem of participation and influence on the political process differently, and his solution is quite different, since he considers the political state outside of, and actually opposite to, public opinion.

Opinion of the public is not expressed by a spatially gathered or communicatively interacting public, but only by an imagined or virtual public. This is why the press plays an important role not only because it delivers information to the public and thus is an important element in the process of public opinion formation, but also because it represents the main "expression means" of the public and thus constitutes the virtual public. According to Tönnies, the "struggle of opinions" that is taking its turn in the public arena (e.g., the media) is not so much a struggle inside the formation of public opinion, where only the "chosen" can participate. Rather, it is a struggle *for* a (primarily "gaseous") opinion of the public, that is, for individuals who will embrace the expressed or published opinion as their own and/or will present it as their own opinion. Since the struggle over opinion is carried on primarily among political parties, it manifests and perpetuates the eternal antagonisms between government and opposition, conservatism and reformism, or orthodox and heterodox orientations. The public watches these fights over opinions like theatergoers, able to see only one side of a scene from an elevated box, because a newspaper presentation is as one-sided as the presentation by parties is partial. Newspapers are not the organs of (opinion of) the public, but rather of political parties that systematically influence them.[30]

Although newspapers are not the only source of information for members of a public, they are, in general, the most important ones. Since newspapers are not independent (in terms of political interests), they often do not allow the public to grasp the truth and may even deceive the public deliberately. Because a public is even less able to "discern and investigate" than journalists, it is also easier misled. However, to be a judge, a public certainly cannot order an investigation; it frequently makes judgments based on hearsay and unconfirmed charges. To achieve greater independence of newspapers, Tönnies is convinced of the need for important press reforms. Following American sociologist J. W. Jenks (1895), he concludes that "we will never have a newspaper which will report completely independently about problems of public life unless we have a newspaper that will be independent of circulation and advertising business" (1922, 184). A temperate assessment of the potential degree of newspapers' independence does not indicate a negation of their role in public opinion processes, since a function of newspapers is that they also (or mainly) allow individuals to *observe* opinion struggles without actively participating.

Tönnies's conception of the public ("large public"), as a social category that is the basis for an opinion of the public, seems to be more adequate (more dialectical, in the first place and, therefore, more universal) than, for instance, the conceptualization in Habermas's theory (both in its earlier version developed in *The Structural Transformation of the Public Sphere* and in his later theory of communicative competence), which is based on the assumption of dialogical competence of individuals. For Habermas, the substance of the public resides in the participation of equal citizens in free public discussion, freed from any conflict of interest (because they left their private interests in the private sphere) and therefore leading to agreement: "Citizens behave like a public when they can discuss issues of common interest without pressure, i.e., assured that they can freely gather and assemble, and freely express and publish their opinions" (Habermas [1962] 1995, 293). The function of newspapers in public discussions should, in principle, involve interpersonal interaction, which was characteristic of the golden age of democracy during antiquity but totally utopian at the time of Tönnies's *Critique,* and even more naive today. Habermas regards new communication and information technologies that have revolutionized communication relations since the middle of the nineteenth century mostly from their negative rather than positive emancipatory potential.[31] Thus, according to Habermas, a public exists already (or merely) when a critical discussion takes place *within it,* as opposed to the presentation of "public status" *before* some type of court, which means the decay of the genuine public. No mediation exists between the two types of the public because they historically exclude each other.

Tönnies, on the other hand, proceeds in his theory from the process of forming and expressing public opinion as a fundamental form of a complex social will in society rather than from the public as a (specific) social category. "The first condition (of an opinion of the public) is a vitality of communication," which is a source of developing thought and judgment (1922, 316, 103). In this sense, all those activities "that liberate a person's tongue, that make him loquacious" are important, specifically exchange, commerce, and political "affairs." These activities require frequent and rapid travel, or "long distance conversation." Thus these activities, along with interpersonal communication, require an intensive transit of people and the transportation of goods, letters, and books.[32] There can be various circumstances for a conversation in community or society, which may unfold among strangers or even enemies, as is often the case in (international) political communication. However, the fundamental condition for expressing and discussing opinion is *freedom of expression,* which is specifically important for the political life of society.

Tönnies (1922, 91–94) stresses the *constitutive role of the form of communication* for the differentiation between community and society. Community is identified by opinion heritage (*Überlieferung*), expressed as passing knowledge from generation to generation (i.e., from older to younger generations) and from higher (predominantly the clergy) to lower strata of society. In contrast, tradition and authority "from upside down" are losing power and giving way to verifiable reason and critique in society. Therefore, written communication and, subsequently, the press became more important than oral communication. In difference to speech—which is always only aimed at and limited by those who are present—the press addresses an unknown and unidentified mass of people. For Tönnies (1922, 220), the difference between community and society is first and foremost constituted by *writing*; as Marx and Engels argued in their *Manifesto*, it was writing that marked the transition from a primeval, classless human community to civilization and class society. At the beginning, books were still characterized by an intimate association between author and reader and by an "exalted" position of the author of literary and scientific texts alike (expressed by a reader's trust, admiration, and gratitude for a writer). Later, the newspaper and its reader meet "on the same level." The newspaper is meant for a large "public" and its influence is not based on an individual point of view or respect. Rather, it influences as "a thing that speaks to the unknown about unknown" and persuades most effectively by "periodic repetition." For this reason, it soon becomes outdated and forgotten. All of this demonstrates the *anonymity* of the author at best and makes us believe that the author is not a concrete person but the newspaper itself.

In addition to political and economic *news* that give a newspaper its name, the reader's "own" newspaper mainly confirms a reader's *views* or, rather, views of friends and those who share a reader's interests and party affiliation, thus strengthening and "encouraging" existing views. Before the appearance of newspapers there were many channels for communicating news; however, the space in which opinions were exchanged and struggled was limited by a physical presence of individuals. The public (*Öffentlichkeit* or *Publikum*)[33] was therefore limited earlier in terms of its size and issues; in the Middle Ages, for example, it was mainly concerned with religious problems and theological discussions. Theologians represented, without doubt, an international, educated public with internal differences in opinion that also suggested social differences among specific classes. The differences became more distinct, and their interests clearer, with the jurisprudential public, although, at that time, discussions between narrow publics never attracted public attention. Debates did not have "a real public which follows struggles with an intense interest, applauds the winner or the favorite with an approval, or scoffs at or insults the opponent, especially when he quits" (Tönnies 1922, 103).

The role Tönnies attributes to the press, or rather to publicity, is to "set the public into motion and to draw it to its side," a process that regularly happens during turbulent times. To achieve this condition, publications present their contents as a genuine public opinion, so that even critics frequently equate the products of publicity with public opinion. Thus the essence of publicity (in contrast to science) is the pursuit of influence, not truth.[34] Occasionally, however, some products of publicity can come even closer to the truth than a scientific statement, according to Tönnies's summary of Wilhelm Bauer's (1914) ideas. Since the beginning, newspapers were not intended only to supplement privately mediated news (i.e., letters), but mostly to spread news that was intended for the public or had escaped censorship.

Following Bauer, Tönnies differentiates between two kinds of publicity, corresponding to "what kind of relationship the publicist has with his own products *(Werke)*." The relationship is natural if a publicist represents his views only out of an internal need created by his own conviction.[35] The other type of publicity follows entirely external motives and impulses. Tönnies adds that this differentiation has actually nothing to do with the distinction between public opinion and the opinion of the public. In fact, Bauer's observations are not convincing for the opinion of the public, according to Tönnies, but fit almost exclusively public opinion. In contrast to science, publicity involves prejudice and bias dealing with state-legislative, political, and economic problems and struggles to influence solely the present (which is illustrative for public opinion). Tönnies even reproaches Bauer, suggesting that "he doesn't have a satisfactory understanding of the properties of a scientific conception" (1916, 420 n.). He is specifically critical of Bauer's differentiation between writing and the press, or between various media, as mere *instances of the same* (1922, 190–193). Bauer's failure becomes seriously problematic when dealing with the press because a newspaper is, in reality, principally "a large capitalist business whose direct and main goal is to create profit in management," and even journalists must conform to this objective (1922, 179–180). Corruption and corporate control are causing a more evident bias of newspapers, so that "independent newspapers" are a total illusion; Tönnies, therefore, considers newspapers to be merely (potential) mediators, and by no means subjects of an opinion of the public. Daily newspapers influence the *gaseous* opinion of the public and vice versa; the narrower and the more solid forms of an opinion of the public are "in a similar relationship of reciprocal influence with a different, more *reliable* literature"—all the way to "the republic of the learned which is the highest instance of opinion of the public in a state or in the 'world,'" and whose members regularly read books (1922, 187). Thus the direction from a "gaseous state" to an intellectual core is a direction in which an opinion achieves greater reliability and solidity.

Tönnies stresses—in opposition to what Habermas asserts later—that opinions are *particular* and *determined by interests* because "the recognizing subjects have their 'human flaws'" (1922, 187). The same opinions frequently indicate the same benefits and interests, and opinion struggles largely demonstrate fights between social strata and classes. Only in science can human recognition—and the opinion it establishes—have a universal quality and a quality of necessity, or at least the latter (an individual and a specific truth). Thus the idea that opinions only depend on human aspiration for knowledge cannot represent a general assumption regarding public opinion or an opinion of the public. Differences in opinions are also, to a certain extent, the result of a different quality of "organs and means of perception." This explains why, for example, less-educated masses often form an agreement more easily than better-educated elites, whose members compete for power and therefore disagree more often. To an even greater extent, differences in opinion result from differences in a subjective life situation (1922, 107). Usual differences in opinion between the city, which is progressive, and the countryside, which is predominantly conservative, can be explained by differences in activities, way of life, and community. Whereas life in the country is calm, stable, and dictated by nature, city life is in constant movement and conditioned by thought and purpose; population density in urban agglomerations by itself stimulates interaction and thinking.

Tönnies assigns the diversity of interests and needs primarily to an *inequality* among those who participate in the process of opinion formation; differences originate in specific *conditions of life, education,* and particular *social groups* and *classes* (1922, 225–226). Similar life conditions activate similar opinions and vice versa: the more the conditions of life are different, the more differentiated opinions become.[36] Tönnies (1922, 46) stresses the fact that ways of speaking and thinking are determined by education and knowledge, and influenced by many people with whom we share life, rank, profession, religion, and political party. He also mentions social-demographic and psychic distinctions (age, gender, development of personality) that regularly determine opinion differences and among them, most of all, social strata and classes. There are always disagreements among opinions of competing groups of political leaders; however, the deepest divisions exist between ruling and subordinate classes, between higher and lower ranks, rich and poor, educated and uneducated. Thus the basic antagonism that is brought forward most notably by (opinion) differences between *political parties* exists between (1) owners and nonowners, rich and poor, capital and work; (2) city and countryside; and (3) the educated and the people (1922, 118). For this reason the opinion of the public can also be wrong: it judges issues according to their image rather than reality, and it can never make use of procedures that a real court or judge uses (1922, 75).

Opinion *formation* is too crucial to be open to everyone's participation, according to Tönnies. However, if an individual cannot participate in the formation of opinion, he should not be prevented from *expressing* an opinion instead of merely *accepting* it (1922, 35). Differentiation between opinion formation and opinion expression is established by the fact that opinion formation belongs to the organic will, whereas opinion expression

tions" and priests "public officials." Tönnies would not entirely agree with this position because of fundamental differences between religion and opinion of the public, although both Dewey and Tönnies share the dialectic of transformation from the private to the public (or vice versa).

Like an opinion of the public, religion also appears in various forms or "aggregate states" in Tönnies's theory (i.e., from a solid to a gaseous one), even though it appears generally that religion is always in a solid state, whereas an opinion of the public primarily appears in gaseous form. When religion represents a counterbalance to dominant ways of thinking about procedures, actions, and their subjects, it looks similar to an opinion of the public, whereas the latter looks similar to religion primarily when it appears as an established way of thought, that is, as part of a "worldview" *(Weltanschauung)*. Tönnies stresses (1922, 232) that we must always compare religion and opinion of the public in their equivalent forms and directions of change to find similarities and differences between these two forms of social will. In general, religion and opinion of the public are constituted in moral judgments; Tönnies suggests "a common and neutral term," *public judgment (das öffentliche Urteil)* (1922, 234) as their common denominator. In his introduction to *Critique* he explains the similarities between the two concepts: "Opinion of the public and religion share—I specifically stress this point—the internally binding power and the obliging will which is often expressed as moral exasperation and intolerance for those who think differently" (1922, vii).

Opinion of the public unites and obliges individuals who produce and accept it, as religion unites and binds believers. Opinion of the public does not just direct individuals to a certain opinion; it also encourages, and even demands, a certain kind of behavior and action, for instance, membership in a political party or reading a specific newspaper. Similarly, religion requires believers to fulfill the requirements of their religious organization. Resemblance between these two forms of social will is most explicit when opinion of the public takes the form of a "patriotic dogma," particularly in the form of revanchism: according to opinion of the public, love for country equals duty, just as love for gods is a religious obligation (1923, 85–86). Nevertheless, the power of religion and opinion of the public do not manifest themselves just internally as oriented connections and unity but, most of all, externally in the relationship with the state. Both religion and opinion of the public struggle for the status of a supreme moral instance and corresponding recognition from the government: every religious denomination wants to become a (state) religion, and every public opinion wants to become an opinion of the public (1923, 87). Opinion of the public often takes paths paved by religion. Moreover, opinion of the public adopted its "means of expression" from religion: in the beginning different kinds of artistic expression, primarily public speech (sermon), and later primarily media connected with writing and presslike books, posters, journals, and, finally, newspapers (1922, 202). This is equally true of public manifestations (proceeding from religious processions) and propaganda. Furthermore, opinion of the public inherited intolerance, and even fanaticism, from religion: both of these forms of social will characteristically argue that an opposing opinion should be "cursed as a sin" (1922, 205; 1923, 87).

Even though both religion and opinion of the public are really "moral judges," they emphasize different subjects. Opinion of the public judges people for their *action* and not for their reasoning or belief; the basis for judgments is the code of *law*. Religion, in contrast, evaluates *convictions* according to *moral* principles. Religion wants to control souls and engage with the most secret beliefs; an opinion of the public sticks to the visible and apparent and, consequently, can be misled by the image. The most significant difference between religion and opinion of the public was established with the economic and political emancipation of the bourgeoisie, which at the end of the seventeenth century and during the eighteenth century found its expression in the first institutions of the public—in English coffee houses, French salons, and German "learned" societies at private meetings, and later in bars. Tönnies explains that

> large differences between religion and opinion of the public become obvious when we imagine the quiet conventions of pious individuals, where belief and godliness are comfortably at home, and on the other side, social gatherings which are extremely important for the formation of opinion of the public: they are the "salon" and the "bar," both are the meeting places of a "world" that thinks, discusses, converses intelligently, and politicizes. (1922, 202)

Tönnies associates the decline of religion and an ever greater role for the opinion of the public (as Dewey did for the public) with the development of *science*. "The progress of opining *[des Meinens]* is primarily a consequence of the influence of advances in scientific knowledge" (1922, 121). In fact, the *scientific* quality not only makes opinion of the public different from religion but turns it into its *opposite*, since religion builds on (blind) belief in an absolute truth. This is the reason why the time of opinion of the public represents "a new era"—the time that affirms scientific and critical ways of thinking. In a way, public opinion is not only mediated by but also subordinated to science: the conveyors of scientific thought— "the learned as teachers"—become direct or indirect, natural and actual leaders of opinion of the public. The more their thought, research, and learning deals with generally important problems, primarily with social, economic, political, and moral or mental questions, the more they fulfill the role of leaders (1922, 207). As leaders of an opinion of the public, Tönnies considers representatives of the profession of teachers as "professional and paid speakers," "free" political speakers and agitators, lawyers, medical doctors, writers (but not poets and other artists whose objective is "to present the un-real as real" and who are therefore just "companions" and rarely leaders of an opinion of the public). The "republic of the learned" who have "educated opinions" constitutes the core of opinion of the public, and the "large public" emerges around them.

Tönnies's discussion of the "republic of the learned" as the core of the public is often seen as an evidence of his reduction of the concept to the intellectual elite and even an ideological "defense of the ruling class in modern society" (Samples 1996, xxi). But Tönnies, as a theorist bound to empirical research, could not escape from *empirical* differences between specific social groups in opinion production and expression, which has no normative implications; he actually predicted the expansion of the public into lower social strata. Moreover, the kind of relationships *historically* established between the forms of social will to specific social classes and groupings represents a fundamental dimension of differentiation between religion and opinion of the public.

Religion is historically rooted in lower social strata; its development is upward toward higher social layers, including priests, artists, and the educated, who give religion its more refined form. In contrast, participation in the formation of an opinion of the public is determined principally by an individual's knowledge, reasoning, education, and political interests. Thus subjects and carriers of public opinion are mostly the bourgeoisie and individuals of rank, men more than women, older people more than younger ones, and those who are personally affected by interests and certain problems more than those who are not (e.g., in economic matters businessmen more than intellectuals, while the reverse is true in intellectual matters). In general, opinion of the public can be defined as an opinion of the educated, in contrast to a "large mass of people" (1923, 91). With the expansion of general and, in particular, political education to lower social strata, the latter become cocreators of opinion of the public, so that opinion of the public, in effect, becomes common and general *(allgemein)*. However, a potential existence of a unified opinion of the public or agreement is thus actually diminished (1922, 229).

Differences and conflicts between religion and public opinion have the character of an ideal type; in the experiential world, religion and public opinion coexist and are intertwined—as are organic and rational wills. This is true for society and community, although historically opinion of the public is gaining power with the affirmation of society, whereas religion is losing it, as Tönnies stresses on several occasions. This does not preclude temporary regressions, that is, abandoning the vision of enlightenment connected with natural-scientific and historiographic knowledge and returning to Christian (Roman Catholic) morals—a "tragic event," according to Tönnies (1922, 571). Still, such regressions are only short-lived experiences of a long-term historical trend in which the opinion of the public will prevail over religious belief.

Tönnies relates the future of religion inversely to the future of opinion of the public developing into a universal *Weltanschauung* that stresses a firm belief in humankind. Incorporating the ideals of religiosity, opinion of the public could move a step closer to a "world religion." Tönnies cites the recognized need for improved economic conditions, for instance, as a way of lifting the spirit of the people *(Volksgeist)*. Social reform is a necessary condition; and Tönnies observes in this connection that "public opinion does not yet risk to accept 'socialism,' but it does no longer dare rejecting it" (1922, 572). His expectations of the decline of the cohesive importance of religion compared to opinion of the public proved to be well justified in later decades, especially with the development of television; his predictions concerning the consequences of an expanding public into lower social strata proved to be true as well.

## "AGGREGATE STATES" OF PUBLIC OPINION

Tönnies makes a further distinction in his discussion of public opinion when he introduces three major states of aggregation that characterize individual as well as social opinions. Following the example of "aggregate states" of matter[37] in the natural sciences, he recognizes the existence of *solid, fluid,* and *gaseous* states, or stages, of public opinion (1922, 257). Drawing on the social-economic, political-legal, and intellectual-moral realms of society—often in a comparative way—he demonstrates the differences among the states of public opinion[38] in terms of characteristic contents of empirical (historical) examples. These three realms correspond to three basic types of *norms* (order, law, and morality), groups of *social values* (economic, political, and mental or intellectual), and types of *human endeavor* (aggregated into the same categories as social values) developed in his general theoretical system in *Gemeinschaft und Gesellschaft*.

The change of aggregate states represents a change in social consciousness that Tönnies calls *Zeitgeist*. The character of this spirit of the time is distinctly international and essentially connected with *doctrines* that represent the form of a simple social will in *Gesellschaft*. Solidity of opinion of the public depends primarily on how unified—politically, or at least mentally and morally—the public is as a carrier of the spirit of the time: the more it constitutes an actual unity, the more its common view and conviction approach the solid opinion of the public (1922, 231). The degree of solidity of opinion of the public is determined by the *degree of unanimity* of the public; thus an aggregate state is actually determined by solidity of opinion and not by the changeable character of the public. His discussion of the various states of public opinion provides a way of distinguishing between highly influential (solid) and minimally effective (gaseous) public opinions and the possibility of change from one state to another; it allows for categorizing a wide variety of social, political, and economic activities that were commonly grouped indiscriminately under public opinion, although they may have differed in strength and endurance. In its solid form, opinion of the public is "a general, firm conviction of the public which, being a carrier of such convictions, represents the whole nation, or even a wider circle of 'civilized humanity'" (1922, 137). The daily public opinion is always under the influence of solid and fluid opinions of the public, which nevertheless does not exclude discord and contradiction among them (1922, 249).

Tönnies defines solid opinion of the public as a kind of agreement over general values, for example, "freedom." Since solid opinion is characterized by reason, tolerance, and the rejection of superstition, it is primarily shaped by intellectuals. Opinion of the public is fluid when, in time, changes occur about controversial issues. A fluid opinion of the public expresses primarily its impartiality; changes can occur because an opinion of the public is unbiased and always stands for what is undeniably expressed in a spirit of common good. Opinion of the public is freed from a zealous assertion of particular interests, which results in a specific, rigidly maintained opinion. A gaseous or ephemeral opinion of the public is superficial and changes rapidly; however, at the same time, it depends on the fluid and, particularly, on the solid opinion of the public. Any historical process that eventually appears as a solid opinion of the public is always molded out of the gaseous state. Nevertheless, the gaseous opinion of the public represents a form of *opinion of the public* because of its congruence with more solid forms, even though it is not clearly differentiated from an inarticulate public opinion in the area of politics. Still, it is exactly the gaseous opinion of the public that most clearly illustrates the dynamics of opinion change, and therefore everyone notices it. However, the power of an opinion of the public is determined primarily by its solid state, which is effective precisely because of its solidity or agreement. Tönnies again borrows a metaphor from physics to state that the *momentum* of the opinion of the public is determined by mass and speed—the power of opinion of the public depends on the degree of its solidity and energy that sets an opinion into motion, hence on a degree of its unanimity and intensity of will.

Solid public opinion must be understood as a steadfast conviction of a public that represents a people or even a larger circle of civilized individuals. An example of a solid public opinion of the public from the social and economic domain is the "idea of personal freedom" that became a solidly anchored ideal. All people love and cherish the specific kind of freedom that they need; thus a slogan is more effective as its potential meanings are more diverse and less specific. The slogan influences reason and will; it has its "material-logical" and "emotional" components, according to Bauer's discussion. "While having only a superficial and weak influence on reason, the effect on the will can be very strong, as is often the case, because mental associations that are released are impregnated with emotions" (Tönnies 1922, 62). But Tönnies disagrees with Bauer by suggesting that this does not mean that "slogans are the only suitable language to communicate with masses . . . because the mass can only think through the images. . . . This should not be appropriate everywhere and always!" A slogan "represents an immense tool for creating a mood, to inflame emotions, to entice conclusions . . . only in connection with certain images and statements about the *facts*" (1922, 63).

In the political sphere, solid elements of opinion of the public are rare, and they are primarily associated with forms of the state. The steadfast solid opinion of the public rejects all that is "feudal" or "barbaric," and, most of all, it rejects theocracy. "Regarding forms of the state and the constitution, political opinion of the public is the more solid, the more these forms are distant from an absolute monarchy, i.e., mostly in democratic republics" (1922, 269). The opinion (characteristic for all civilized states) that the essence of the state resides in acting for the good of individuals, is one of the solid elements of opinion of the public which is most prominent in republics (1922, 270).

In intellectual and moral areas, the basic feature of a solid opinion of the public is rationality *(Vernünftigkeit)*, an expression of a general struggle for knowledge and freedom. Opinion of the public is struggling against remnants of the "dark ages"; conceptions and opinions, in general, characterize this "darkness" as superstition, which also represents a "basic element of positive religions as a power of a social will" (1922, 279). Thus Tönnies, referring to his own time, maintains that the opinion of the public repudiates the existence of the devil, sorcery, and magic. According to him, radical change regarding opinion about these and other phenomena could only have emerged for two reasons: (1) change is a consequence of research acceptable among enlightened people, even though they are unable to verify the evidence personally, or (2) people are affected by the *Zeitgeist,* by the "gradual, invisible, but, nevertheless, serious remodeling of the prevailing mental orientation" (1922, 282). The prevailing conviction about the accuracy of a scientific view does not create an opinion of the public by itself; what is important is that a rejection of such a view is subjected to a moral condemnation and the view itself is accepted as morally valuable, that is, as a source of progress and culture.

The contradiction of opinion of the public lies in the fact that it requires freedom of thought, speech, and press, on one hand, while on the other it is "as a social will, a power that unites its members and obliges them; it applies the principle of tolerance to differences in religious opinion, as being of minor importance, and definitely not to others, primarily political differences, where it most of the time acts as being on its own turf" (1922, 285). Nevertheless, opinion of the public does not demand obedience from those who assume leading positions but only recognition of the "correct" and "fair" opinions or at least nonresistance.

The state of *fluid* public opinion, according to Tönnies, could also be understood as short-lived public opinion, made for the day and therefore less stable, since it was also formed without the support of a solid public opinion. Instead, this type of public opinion is to be seen as consisting of partial opinions, formed, joined, and generalized often in opposition to the solid public opinion. For Tönnies, the most important example of the fluid public opinion, located in social and economic life, is respect for "work." The evaluation of work changes significantly through time. For the nineteenth-century bourgeoisie, the value of work was juxtaposed to "*Junkers* and priests," although it valued as "work" only commercial and industrial activities that reflected productivity and profits. Physical and manual work were discounted and actually descended the social ladder with the augmentation of a class of wage workers (1922, 262). The other subjects used by Tönnies to delineate the fluid public opinion of his time are women and the women's movement.

After World War I, Tönnies identified a typical case of a fluid public opinion in the political sphere in Germany: the attitude toward the German monarchy and constitution, which determined the rights of "the crown" and the "representation of the people." Before the war, public opinion supported a limited monarchy but after it increasingly favored a parliamentary form of government. Based on this example, Tönnies ex-

**Table 2  Differences in Content of the Three "Aggregate States" of Opinion of the Public**

| Layers of public opinion | Spheres | | |
| | Social and economic | Political and legal | Intellectual and moral |
| --- | --- | --- | --- |
| Solid | Freedom | Forms of state | Rationality |
| Fluid | Work | Monarchy | Moral questions |
| Gaseous | Equality | Daily press | "Court of public opinion" |

plains that the fluid public opinion can be "transformed" or, rather, that even "rigid prejudices and views" can be changed if an "appropriate power"—agitation and advertising—is used (1922, 273). Differently seen, fluidity is a consequence of the fact that an opinion of the public is always impartial—not determined by the interests of a political party. It supports what is "undeniably in a spirit of common good and what guarantees a better future. This is how it justifies the changes to itself and to the world; its frequently abrupt turn reminds of the changes in fashion, like clothing, furniture, etc." (1922, 273).

In general, law and morals are the easiest sphere in which to observe the differences between solid and fluid public opinions. As for the process of punishment, its methods, and course, public opinion is solid by rejecting torture and horrifying methods of execution; it is fluid regarding all other kinds of physical punishment or the death sentence itself. Public opinion solidly demands the sharpest punishment for certain kinds of crimes (e.g., sex offenses) but is fluid regarding trials of juvenile delinquents.

The *gaseous (ephemere)* public opinion has several characteristics. According to Tönnies, it is highly unstable; it appears and disappears because it frequently changes the objects of its attention. It could be observed in cities like Paris, an urban society where public attention was easily distracted and shifted from one subject to be focused on something else. This state of public opinion is also fast moving and hastily established. The daily or gaseous public opinion is largely determined by fluid, but primarily by solid, forms of public opinion; it appears "as their application to specific cases and occasions" (1922, 264). Although public opinion opposed slavery and the remnants of a feudal order (e.g., serfdom) at the beginning of the eighteenth century, many forms of slavery (United States) and serfdom (Russia) continued during the nineteenth century. In Tönnies's time, public opinion only rarely opposed violations against social equality and more often disapproved of militarism—as was the case with the Dreyfus affair in France. Nevertheless, Tönnies emphasizes that none of this dissatisfaction with social and economic events gives public opinion a political character; instead, its attention may be directed toward internal reforms. However, it never turns against the form of the state or the constitution which have produced a high degree of solidity of public opinion for some time.

On the whole, the gaseous public opinion about political issues is the most manifest form. It is intertwined with the opinion of the public—understood as a unified collective person *(einheitliche Gesamtperson)*—and with public opinion as a unity of different expressed opinions. It is the latter that is meant when the press is spoken of as an organ or an instrument of public opinion. However, the daily press is simultaneously

> the most important "means of expression" of opinion of the public also as a unified social will. . . . The assumption is that opinion of the public exists outside the daily press and independent from it and that by publishing a fact or an event it is formed as if by the necessity of a natural law, and later surfaces unanimously in the daily press, as well as in other media. In this case, newspapers will be unanimous, or at least 'in tune;' the partisan views they otherwise support will retreat, become subordinate, and serve the opinion of the public. (Tönnies 1922, 276)

Tönnies thinks of an opinion of the public in such a situation as a hurricane that destroys all obstacles in its path and always struggles for a clear and decisive judgment. This is most obvious in such distinct cases when events or persons who represent a specific moral phenomenon have to be judged and elicit either general approval or disapproval; these are the "cases when it becomes obvious that 'it's morally self-evident'" (1922, 277). In the cases involving political events and persons, the opinion of the public becomes politically relevant; discoveries about morally controversial events in a politician's private life should be less important than political errors, which can be "criticized more from an intellectual point of view than from a moral perspective" (1922, 277).

The gaseous opinion of the public in the intellectual and moral sphere has similar features to that in the political and legal sphere, according to Tönnies. It is here that the opinion of the public attracts attention most often and vigorously. Consequently, it appears as if its essence is created in this sphere. The opinion of the public acts as a moral judge and in this function reacts negatively as a "penal court." Since the opinion of the public has the same function in the first two spheres—the social-economic and the legal-political—this capacity should be considered its distinguishing function. Similar to the legal-political sphere, here the opinion of the public can be misread for public opinion, since in special cases (i.e., dealing with an important public figure) the public opinion of a specific class or place can change into an opinion of the public. The reverse is true as well, namely, that the opinion of the public always represents "some" public opinion.

The dialectical character of the opinion of the public is undeniable not only because it appears in different aggregate states, but also because it can develop from public opinion, although the latter idea is not theoretically elaborated by Tönnies. Agitation and propaganda[39] disseminate and strengthen opinions, and in favorable circumstances they can accomplish the development of collective opinion *(Gesamtmeinung)* from a partial one *(Teilmeinung)*, that is, an opinion of the public can develop from a partisan public opinion, as well as a dominant opinion from a subordinate one (1922, 200). In general, opinions tend to strengthen in the course of time, gain power, and even become self-evident; this applies to an individual as well as to a nation or group of nations. With age, opinion approaches faith. On the other hand, with time, "respect diminishes" and critique becomes stronger: "the young are always inclined to laugh at old age, and this inclination offsets an otherwise more efficient inclination to respect it" (1922, 200). Consequently, with time even the most solid opinion fades away, mostly because of insufficient action.

Tönnies's discussions of the "empirical characteristics of the ephemeral opinion of the public" or "the daily opinion of the public" reveal that in its lowest "aggregate state," opinion of the public has been practically devoid of what essentially defined it at the pure level of conceptualization. It is like a "not very polite child" characterized by (1) rapid variability, (2) inconsistency, (3) superficiality, (4) lack of criticism, (5) burden of prejudices, (6) consistent return to the "original state," and (7) vitality of prejudices about people (more than about objects). According to Tönnies, we can recognize an opinion of the public even in its gaseous state because (8) even though it rarely corresponds to the idea of a mental form of a rational social will, a gaseous opinion of the public nevertheless perceives emotions to which it submits, as being alien; (9) even the gaseous opinion of the public expresses ideas that can be found also in its fluid and solid states, especially in the moral sphere; (10) the gaseous opinion of the public can be easily recognized because it makes use of slogans; (11) slogans are effectively used primarily by political parties, and hence the public as a subject of the opinion of the public can be identified as a "generalized party" that became, like many others, a "winning" party; and (12) a certain education and "intellect" (albeit average) are characteristic even for the gaseous opinion of the public. Political education is particularly low and, even though its level differs among groups and nations, this typically results in leveling the national (general) interest with partisan and class interests (1922, 245–253). Nevertheless, in spite of these features, Tönnies suggests that in the "daily opinion of the public," or rather in the "daily public opinion,"[40] which is always the most visible since it is expressed in newspapers, it is impossible to detect its state as (only) a public opinion or (already) an opinion of the public.

## THE FUTURE OF PUBLIC OPINION

For Tönnies, the public and the opinion of the public are, in the first place, normative concepts (i.e., ideal abstractions) and, at the same time, ideals

respect to political matters. He even suggests that "public opinion is easily accessible to these influences because it is itself a spiritual force" ([1923] 1971, 262). The use of the word, the printed word through the press, in particular, becomes their most effective instrument.

Looking at the question of power, he agrees that the power of the press "is more obvious than the power of public opinion" ([1923] 1971, 254). He describes the political, economic, and intellectual forces, constituting another kind of elite that often stands behind the modern press. Since "industrial capital" had become a major influence, even more powerful than landed estate, Tönnies argues that it also regulates the power of the press because (1) it more directly reflects the spirit of modernity; (2) it is closely related to the world of information and communication, and national and international politics; (3) the press itself is a capitalist enterprise based on advertising, and (4) "in line with the great body of literature inasmuch as it is carried along by the progress of scientific thinking and stands in the service of a predominantly liberal and religiously as well as politically progressive consciousness" ([1923] 1971, 255–356).

Tönnies suggests that in the competition among capitalist ideas a capitalist press is, theoretically at least, in the position of refusing access to other capitalist powers only as long as those forces manage to gain control of the press. Citing examples of corruption in a capitalist press system through monopoly ownership and corporation control, he interprets these developments as more general expressions of the corruption of public life in the United States. Although he acknowledges the work of press critics, he predicts that their independent voices will eventually disappear, or will yield to the dictates of conglomerates and monopolies instead of reflecting public opinions. Tönnies lists a number of American sources to support his arguments, among them Edward A. Ross, who had stated in 1920 that the sellout of newspapers to business interests had never been as widespread as at that time, and Lester Ward, who had called newspapers organs of deception: "Every prominent newspaper is the defender of some interest and everything it says is directly or indirectly (and most effective when indirect) in support of that interest. There is no such thing at the present time as a newspaper that defends a principle" (1922, 184).

Tönnies criticizes the use of modern communication media by special interest groups, governments, and others, as well as their mode of operation (focused on business practices), because in that process "judgments and opinion are wrapped up like grocers' good and offered for consumption in their objective reality" ([1887] 1963, 221). But he also recognizes the *potential* power of a modern press system, and he does not confine it to a particular country; on the contrary, he envisions a worldwide influence, a force capable of uniting others and establishing a world power. He explains that the press

> in its tendencies and potentialities, is definitely international, thus comparable to the power of a permanent or temporary alliance of states. It can, therefore, be conceived as its ultimate aim to abolish the multiplicity of states and substitute for it a single world market, which would be ruled by thinkers, scholars, and writers and could dispense with means of coercion other than those of a psychological nature. ([1887] 1963, 221)

He concludes that, although unlikely, recognition of these tendencies "serves to assist in the understanding of many phenomena of the real world and to the realization of the fact that the existence of natural states is but a temporary limitation of the boundaryless *Gesellschaft* ([1887] 1963, 221).

He cites the United States as an example of a modern society that "can or will least of all claim a truly national character" ([1887] 1963, 221). Tönnies concludes that the press must be understood as an instrument of liberal thought, a force used to exert influence on more conservative elements in society; this assessment implied an allegiance with ideas of less "church-oriented religiosity" and "an agnostic world view connected with the natural sciences" ([1923] 1971, 256).

Tönnies discusses the overriding effects of liberalism, making it a "constitutive part of public opinion everywhere, except in areas of cultural transition" (1922, 257) and finds that, given the development of the modern age, the press had become a protection and defense of liberal ideas.

The future of public opinion, its rise, perhaps, to a "world religion" and its role as the social conscience of mankind, must be accompanied by improvements in the communication system. Since the press would continue to play an important part in the dissemination of ideas, Tönnies envisions the establishment of an independent press. His suggestions are based on the writings of German–American journalist Ferdinand Hansen (1922, 574),[41] who had advocated the creation of a completely independent press system with newspapers that could rely on an independent news service and were financially free, supported by large circulation rather than by advertising.

In 1920s America, Edward C. Hayes also demanded that newspapers give priority to ideas that emerge in free discussion and not to money: newspapers should be forced by law to assign equal space to each of the four parties that were the most powerful in last elections (Wilson 1962, 81). Essentially, Tönnies considers these suggestions significant for Germany, similar to Bauer's appeals to stop sensationalism and the violation of "the sanctity of private life." Nevertheless, as much as these goals seem significant, they also seem *unrealizable*. The proposals are valuable, however, because they are counterfactual and educative, that is, they call critical attention to the negative facts in the press which, according to Tönnies, can only be reformed *from the inside*: "The need for such a reform should be set in motion through *public opinion,* which would be an effective, perhaps the most effective means of self-education for *the opinion of the public,*" as Tönnies ends his *Kritik der öffentlichen Meinung* (1922, 575).

Through published writings about the press and in his role in the German Sociological Association, Tönnies had contact with representatives of *Zeitungswissenschaft,* the science of the press, who jealously protected their own qualitative and quantitative investigations of the press. He rejected the separation of media studies from sociology, for instance, as well as the accusation that he did not like *Zeitungswissenschaft* as a field of special inquiry. In a response to Emil Dovifat, a founding father of "the science of the press," he stated that the advocates of *Zeitungswissenschaft* could make highly valuable contributions to a *critical* history of the press, especially from philosophical and sociological points of view. He expresses the hope—and he included those who represented *Zeitungswissenschaft* with his reference to a lack of a critical approach to press studies—that the cooperation between sociology and *Zeitungswissenschaft* might contribute toward a liberation of "press scientists" from the press, in general, and from party affiliations and dependence on respective newspapers in particular (1931a, 72–74). He elaborates his position vis-à-vis *Zeitungswissenschaft* again in a letter published early in 1931, in which he denied the charge that he wanted to define the study of the press as an exclusive part of sociology. He feels that the investigation of the press constitutes an important area of sociography (i.e., empirical sociology) and suggests that the treatment of literature must be part of defining its significance for the social life of a people; newspapers were part of this literature. He also blames the failure of an intense sociological study of press systems on the newness of sociology as a discipline in Germany (1931b, 1–2).[42]

When the 1930 convention of the German Sociological Association included a debate concerning the press and public opinion, Tönnies expresses his disappointment over the fact that none of the speakers had offered a systematic treatment of the press as a capitalistic enterprise, since the production of news had created a powerful social force in German society. He comments on the dangers of interfering in the process of communication by advertisers and the threats to journalistic freedom of expression. But he also wonders how free opinions really were, how they were related to other opinions, and how close they came to other "verified" opinions present in other areas of social life. He specifically refers to opinions of educated individuals whose contributions to social policy and reform were needed. Yet their ideas either were reflected in a distorted manner or were rarely published. Tönnies mentions national economists,

among them Brentano, Schmoller, Wagner, and Knapp, whose opinions—
because they were close enough to be identified with socialistic ideas—
had become suspect in the eyes of the bourgeois and, in particular, the
Catholic press. He concludes, almost despairingly, that "when men and
women of this caliber are dead, they may receive rather beautiful obitu-
aries; as long as they live, they find themselves pushed to the wall and
rarely listened to; that is an experience, which I want to emphasize on the
basis of my long life"(1931a, 74).

In summary, Tönnies provides an extensive, in-depth discussion of
communication phenomena, public opinion, and the press as part of his
effort to develop a broad sociological framework beginning with *Gemeinschaft und Gesellschaft*. In this context, he presents a detailed historical
analysis of the concept of public opinion and a definition that takes into
account the dynamic nature of his own conceptual scheme of societal development and gives preference to the complex processes in culture and
society over their institutionalized forms in politics and the state. He
seems particularly concerned with the rise of public opinion and media
power and comments on the dangers inherent in the capitalistic nature of
the press in modern society. His differentiation between the state, the society, and the public actually represents the roots of the productive idea
(developed later by Gramsci) of the exclusion of the economic sphere (because of the specific power of capital) from civil society, both being opposed to the state.

Tönnies's ideas concerning the rise of public opinion to a universal social conscience vis-à-vis religion and the role of the press in an evolution-
ary schema suggest a novel approach to popular culture phenomena and
represent one of the most significant classical social-theoretical contributions to the field. Unfortunately, theories originating at the beginning of
the twentieth century seem to be much less influential than more practical-minded empirical approaches developed after the 1930s and are
presently almost completely "forgotten." The contributions by Tönnies
and other early sociological conceptualizations of public opinion also
demonstrate that, as Horst Pöttker (1993, 213) suggests, "leaving aside the
abundance of data gathered during more than six decades of empirical
communication research, the notion of a continuous progress in theory is
apparently not very appropriate." Similarly, in the late 1950s, Harold
Lasswell (1957, 34–35) admitted that since the nineteenth century, no
progress in public opinion research has been achieved at the theoretical
level; rather, the progress was only instrumental. Forty decades later,
Lasswell's (self)critical assessment still holds true. Thus Tönnies's systematic analysis of public opinion in relation to other forms of a (complex)
social will still represents a valuable critical challenge to public opinion
theory and media research; beginning with his demand for a systematic

# REFERENCES

Albig, William. [1939] 1956. *Modern Public Opinion*. New York: McGraw–Hill.

Arato, Andrew, and Jean L. Cohen. 1996. "The Rise, Decline, and Reconstruction of the Concept of Civil Society." *Politicna dumka–Political Thought* (Kiev) 1: 134–138.

Arendt, Hannah. [1958] 1989. *The Human Condition*. Chicago: University of Chicago Press.

Bauer, Wilhelm. 1914. *Die öffentliche Meinung und ihre geschichtlichen Grundlagen*. Tübingen: Mohr.

Bauer, Wilhelm. [1933] 1963. "Public Opinion." In *Encyclopedia of the Social Sciences*, edited by E. R. A. Seligman, 669–674. New York: Macmillan.

Bluntschli, Johann Caspar, Karl Brater et al. 1862. *Deutsches Staatswörterbuch*. 11 vols. 1857–1870.

Bücher, Karl. 1901. "The Genesis of Journalism." In *Industrial Evolution*, 242–243. New York: Holt.

Bücher, Karl. 1926. *Gesammelte Aufsätze zur Zeitungskunde*. Tübingen: Lauppsche Buchhandlung.

Bryce, James. 1921. *Modern Democracies*. New York: Macmillan.

Bryce, James. [1888] 1995. *The American Commonwealth*. 2 vols. Indianapolis: Liberty Fund.

Cahnman, W. Jacob, ed. 1973. *Ferdinand Tönnies: A New Evaluation*. Leiden: Brill.

Cahnman, W. Jacob, and Rudolf Heberle, eds. 1971. *Ferdinand Tönnies on Sociology: Pure, Applied, and Empirical*. Chicago: University of Chicago Press.

Dewey, John. [1927] 1991. *The Public and Its Problems*. Athens: Swallow.

Freund, Julien. 1978. "German Sociology in the Time of Max Weber." In *A History of Sociological Analysis*, edited by T. Bottomore and R. Nisbet, 149–186. New York: Basic.

Gälli, Anton. 1977. *100 Years of Mass Communication in Germany*. Munich: Institute for Economic Research.

Glasser, T. Lewis, and Charles T. Salmon, eds. 1995. *Public Opinion and the Communication of Consent*. New York: Guilford.

Gollin, L. Gillian, and Albert E. Gollin. 1973. "Tönnies on Public Opinion." In *Ferdinand Tönnies: A New Evaluation*, edited by W. J. Cahnman, 181–203. Leiden: Brill.

Habermas, Jürgen. [1964] 1979. The Public Sphere. *Communication and Class Struggle*. Vol.1, *Capitalism, Imperialism*, edited by A. Mattelart and S. Siegelaub, 198–201. New York: International General.

Habermas, Jürgen. [1962] 1995. *The Structural Transformation of the Public Sphere: An Inquiry into a Category of Bourgeois Society*. Cambridge: MIT Press.

Hardt, Hanno. 1979. *Social Theories of the Press: Early German and American Perspectives*. Beverly Hills: Sage.

Hegel, Georg Wilhelm Friedrich. [1821] 1971. *Philosophy of Right*. Translated with notes by T. M. Knox. London: Oxford University Press.

Jenks, Jeremiah W. 1895. "The Guidance of Public Opinion." *American Journal of Sociology* 1, no. 2: 158–169.

Kant, Immanuel. [1781] 1952. *The Critique of Pure Reason.* Chicago: Encyclopaedia Britannica.

Keane, John. 1982. "Elements of a Radical Theory of Public Life: From Tönnies to Habermas and Beyond." *Canadian Journal of Political and Social Theory* 3: 11–49.

Keane, John. 1984. *Public Life and Late Capitalism: Toward a Socialist Theory of Democracy.* Cambridge: Cambridge University Press.

Knies, Karl. 1857. *Der Telegraph als Verkehrsmittel: Mit Erörterungen über den Nachrichtenverkehr Überhaupt.* Tübingen: Lauppsche Buchhandlung.

Lasswell, Harold D. 1957. "The Impact of Public Opinion in Our Society." *Public Opinion Quarterly* 21, no. 1: 33–38.

Lippmann, Walter. 1925. *The Phantom Public.* New York: Harcourt, Brace.

Lippmann, Walter. [1922] 1960. *Public Opinion.* New York: Macmillan.

Löbl, Emil. 1903. *Kultur und Presse.* Leipzig: Duncker & Humblot.

Loomis, Charles P., John C. McKinney. 1996. Introduction to *Community & Society,* by F. Tönnies, 1–30, 273–283 (notes). New Brunswick, N.J.: Transaction.

MacKinnon, William A. [1828] 1971. *On the Rise, Progress, and Present State of Public Opinion, in Great Britain, and Other Parts of the World.* Shannon: Irish University Press.

Marx, Karl. [1842] 1969. "Die Verhandlungen des 6. rheinischen Landtags." In *Pressefreiheit und Zensur,* by K. Marx and F. Engels, 44–99. Frankfurt: Europäische Verlagsanstalt.

Marx, Karl. [1867] 1973. *Das Kapital, Marx–Engels Werke.* Vol. 23–25. Berlin: Dietz.

Masuda, Yoneji. [1980] 1983. *The Information Society as Post–Industrial Society.* Washington, D.C.: World Future Society.

Merz–Benz, Peter–Ulrich. 1995. *Tiefsinn und Scharfsinn: Ferdinand Tönnies' begriffliche Konstitution der Sozialwelt.* Frankfurt: Suhrkamp.

Neidhardt, Friedhelm, ed. 1994. *Öffentlichkeit, öffentliche Meinung, soziale Bewegungen: Kölner Zeitschrift für Soziologie.* Sonderheft 34. Opladen: Westdeutscher Verlag.

Noelle–Neumann, Elisabeth. 1974. "The Spiral of Silence: A Theory of Public Opinion." *Journal of Communication* 24, no. 2: 43–51.

Noelle–Neumann, Elisabeth. [1980] 1993. *The Spiral of Silence: Public Opinion–Our Social Skin.* Chicago: University of Chicago Press.

Palmer, Paul A. 1938. "Ferdinand Tönnies's Theory of the Public Opinion." *Public Opinion Quarterly* 2, no. 4: 584–595.

Park, Robert E. [1904] 1972. *The Crowd and the Public.* Edited by H. Elsner Jr. Chicago: University of Chicago Press.

Pöttker, Horst. 1993. "Ferdinand Tönnies und die Schweigespirale: Zur Mutation einer Theorie über die öffentliche Meinung." In *Theorien öffentlicher Kommunikation: Problemfelder, Positionen, Perpektiven,* edited by G. Bentele and M. Rühl, 203–213. Munich: Olschläger.

Rousseau, Jean-Jacques. [1762] 1947. *The Social Contract.* Translated by C. Frankel. New York: Hafner.

Rudolph, Günther. 1995. *Die philosophisch–soziologischen Grundpositionen von Ferdinand Tönnies: Ein Beitrag zur Geschichte und Kritik der bürgerlichen Soziologie.* Hamburg: Rolf Fechner.

Samples, John. 1996. Introduction to the Transaction edition, in *Community and Society*, by F. Tönnies, xi–xxvi. New Brunswick, N.J.: Transaction.

Schäffle, Albert E. F. 1881. *Bau und Leben des Sozialen Körpers*. Vol. 1. Tübingen: Lauppsche Buchhandlung.

Schmidtchen, Gerhard. 1959. *Die befragte Nation: Über den Einfluss der Meinungsforschung auf die Politik*. Freiburg: Romabach.

Splichal, Slavko. 1999. *Public Opinion: Developments and Controversies in the Twentieth Century*. Lanham, Md.: Rowman & Littlefield.

Tocqueville, Alexis de. [1840] [1912] 1995. *Democracy in America*. http://darwin.clas.virginia.edu/(tsawyer/DETOC. Originally scanned and corrected by Thomas G. Roche at the University of Virginia (June 15, 1995) from *Democracy in America*, by Alexis de Tocqueville; translated by Henry Reeve. New York: Appleton, 1912.

Tönnies, Ferdinand. 1896. *Hobbes' Leben und Lehre*. Stuttgart: Friedrich Frommanns Verlag/E. Hauff.

Tönnies, Ferdinand. 1909. *Die Sitte*. Frankfurt: Literarische Anstalt, Rütten & Loening.

Tönnies, Ferdinand. 1916. "Zur Theorie der öffentlichen Meinung." *Schmollers Jahrbuch für Gesetzgebung, Verwaltung, und Volkswirtschaft im Deutschen Reiche* 40, no. 4: 2001–2030.

Tönnies, Ferdinand. 1922. *Kritik der öffentlichen Meinung*. Berlin: Verlag von Julius Springer.

Tönnies, Ferdinand. 1923. "Macht und Wert der Öffentlichen Meinung." In *Die Dioskuren: Jahrbuch für Geisteswissenschaften* 2: 72–95. Translated in *Ferdinand Tönnies—On Sociology: Pure, Applied, and Empirical*. Edited by W. J. Cahnman and R. Heberle. Chicago: University of Chicago Press, 1971.

Tönnies, Ferdinand. 1925. "Einteilung der Soziologie." *Zeitschrift für die gesamte Staatswissenschaft* 79: 1. Translated in *Ferdinand Tönnies—On Sociology: Pure, Applied, and Empirical*. Edited by W. J. Cahnman and R. Heberle. Chicago: University of Chicago Press, 1971.

Tönnies, Ferdinand. 1926. *Das Eigentum*. Vienna: W. Braumüller.

Tönnies, Ferdinand. 1927. "Amerikanische Soziologie." *Weltwirtschaftliches Archiv* 26, no. 2: 1–10.

Tönnies, Ferdinand. 1928. "Die öffentliche Meinung in unserer Klassik." *Archive für Buchgewerbe und Gebrauchsgraphik* 4: 31–49.

Tönnies, Ferdinand. 1929. "Statistik und Soziographie." *Allgemeines Statistisches Archiv* 18: 546–558. Translated in *Ferdinand Tönnies—On Sociology: Pure, Applied, and Empirical*. Edited by W. J. Cahnman and R. Heberle. Chicago: University of Chicago Press, 1971.

Tönnies, Ferdinand. 1931. *Einführung in die Soziologie*. Stuttgart: Ferdinand Enke. As reported by E. G. Jacoby, "Three Aspects of the Sociology of Tönnies." In *Ferdinand Tönnies: A New Evaluation*. Edited by Werner Cahnman. Leiden: Brill, 1973.

Tönnies, Ferdinand. 1931a. "Verhandlungen des siebten deutschen Soziologentages, 28 September bis 1 Oktober 1930." *Schriften der deutschen Gesellschaft für Soziologie, 1. Serie: Verh.d.dtsch. Soziologentage*. Vol. 1. Tübingen: Mohr/Paul Siebeck.

Tönnies, Ferdinand. 1931b. "Offene Antwort." *Zeitungswissenschaft* 6, no. 1: 1–2.

Tönnies, Ferdinand. 1932. Open letter in *Schleswig-Holsteinische Volkszeitung*, Kiel, 29 July 1932. Translated in *Ferdinand Tönnies on Sociology: Pure, Applied, and Empirical*. Edited by W. J. Cahnman and R. Heberle. Chicago: University of Chicago Press, 1971.

Tönnies, Ferdinand. 1932a. "Mein Verhältnis zur Soziologie." In *Soziologie von Heute*, edited by R. Thurnwald, 103–122. Leipzig: Hirschfeld. Translated in *Ferdinand Tönnies on Sociology: Pure, Applied, and Empirical*. Edited by W. J. Cahnman and R. Heberle. Chicago: University of Chicago Press, 1971.

Tönnies, Ferdinand. [1887] 1963. *Community and Society*. Translated and edited by C. Loomis. New York: Harper Torchbooks.

Tönnies, Ferdinand. [1887] 1991. *Gemeinschaft und Gesellschaft*. Darmstadt: Wissenschaftliche Buchgesellschaft.

Wilson, Francis Graham. 1962. *A Theory of Public Opinion*. Chicago: Regnery.

Wirth, Louis. 1948. "Consensus and Mass Communication." *American Sociological Review* 13, no. 1: 1–15.

United States, while Edward Bernays published *Crystallizing Public Opinion* in 1923.

Although the selections that follow avoid as much as possible purely descriptive accounts and extensive historical passages, the reader will nevertheless encounter the author's preference for detailed examples, mostly of a historical or political nature.

The selections translated are from chapter 1, "Meinen und Meinung," section 2, "Grundverhältnisse der Begriffe" (excerpts), pages 11–12, 19–20, 23; chapter 2, "Gemeinsame Meinungen," section 1, "Bedingungen der Gemeinsamkeit," (excerpts), pages 25–26, 27–28, 30–37 (in "Opining and Opinion, Common Opinions"); chapter 3, Öffentliche Meinung," section 1, "Das öffentliche Wesen" (excerpts) pages 87–90; section 2, "Nachrichten und Öffentlichkeit," pages 91–100 (in "Public Opinion"); chapter 4, "Öffentliche Meinung und 'die' Öffentliche Meinung," section 1, "Entstehung und Charakter der Öffentlichen Meinung," pages 131–147; section 2, "Näheres über politische Kämpfe" (excerpts), pages 174–175, 177–178; section 3, "Vulgäre Erscheinung der Öffentlichen Meinung," pages 178–189; section 4, "Höhere Erscheinungen der öffentlichen Meinung," pages 189–215 (in "Public Opinion and 'the' Public Opinion"); chapter 5, "Die öffentliche Meinung und ihre Merkmale," section 1, "Soziologische Zusammenhänge der Öffentlichen Meinung" (excerpts), pages 219–222; section 2, "Soziologische Wechselwirkungen" (excerpts), pages 228–232; 234–235; 238–239; 245–256 (in "Public Opinion and Its Characteristics"); chapter 7, "Macht und Machtfaktoren der Öffentlichen Meinung," section 1, "Die Macht" (excerpts), pages 299–301 (in "Power As a Factor of Public Opinion"); chapter 8, "Die Öffentliche Meinung als Faktor des Staatslebens," section 1, "Insgemein und in Amerika" (excerpts), pages 321–322, 355–359 (in "Public Opinion as a Political Factor in the Life of the State"); chapter 11, "Die Zukunft der Öffentlichen Meinung," pages 569–575 (in "The Future of Public Opinion").

The selections follow the order of the original book chapters. They introduce Tönnies's terminology, his concepts of public opinion and "the" Public Opinion, and his basic sociological theory and terminology related to notions of community and society to reflect the logical organization of his ideas. The translations of specific concepts, like *Wesenwille* and *Kürwille*, for instance, follow Tönnies's article on philosophical terminology (1899) and differ from translations used in the opening essays of this book because this translation follows Tonnies's own inconsistencies in his application of these concepts and does not attempt any correction.

Tönnies's style of writing is convoluted and sometimes complex, his sentences are long and involved, and they often approximate a conversational tone. The use of language itself reflects his times and the conventions of his era; indeed, some words are outdated and unknown to the contemporary German reader. Although an effort has been made to maintain his sense of dedication and the intensity of argument that characterizes his formulations of public opinion, the following translation is a modernized version of his text. Additions or corrections are bracketed [. . .] in the text, and references to names or works have been completed and added (whenever possible) in chapter 8 (following the notes). Finally, the translation retains the gender bias of the original as a historical condition of the time and a reflection of Tönnies's expression in particular.

# 1

## Opining and Opinion, Common Opinions

### OPINING AND OPINION, SECTION TWO. BASIC CONCEPTS

**11. (The Concept of Opinion).** To examine the concept of opinion we must maintain the meaning it shares with corresponding words in Latin and the romance languages: this meaning is an intellectual one that we want to place in the foreground of a definition of the German verb *meinen*. It is a meaning that other languages normally indicate with words such as "thinking," "believing," and "conjecturing."

Keeping in mind the previous supporting discussions of language, we can summarize that thinking and opining exist in a threefold relationship to wishing and wanting, or to feelings in general. (1) The former emerge by and large from the latter, they are co-determined, they express feelings; (2) because of this and as a consequence, thinking and opining contain an emphasis on emotion; "wanting" or "not wanting" stand for an affirmative or negative, favorable or unfavorable judgment; (3) thinking and opining are essentially as perfect as wanting: opining = having an opinion, having formed an opinion is like wanting = having decided, intending. However, like all acts of having and possessing, opining and wanting too obligate the soul in two ways: (1) they immediately affect the process of becoming, that is, future opinions and decisions—as movements are a result of impulses; (2) they are also effective against resisting ideas and tendencies as a form of coercion—with the aid of memory. One is reminded of what one "actually means," "actually wants," which is sufficient—and actually normal for weaker dispositions—for giving thought and will a specific, normal direction. Consequently, a firm conviction, but also a firm will—the basis for action, at least of an individual with character, of whom one can say that he "has an opinion" or a will—commits and controls. In this sense one praises the individual who has "the courage of his opinion," and obtaining an opinion, or even "forming" one's own opinion becomes an accomplishment, that is, an arbitrary practice that is troublesome and time consuming.

[. . .]

19. (Concepts, Believing, Opining). All thinking individuals have and harbor certain "views" about so-called spiritual and human matters, about natural phenomena and those of culture, past, present, and future; they are more or less determined, more or less firm and decided "views." When these views are called "opinions," the term refers to their variety and difference and, therefore, to their subjectivity, which suggests their frequent disagreement and opposition to each other. In fact, they exclude each other so that only one of them may be "correct" while the other one must be "false," unless both of them are incorrect. These are attributes used to judge opinions, measures of correctness, which are conceptualized like a straight line, a mathematical measure, and therefore constitute scientific concepts. Correct are those opinions which—according to one's opinion—agree with the facts; thus it is just another expression for approving or "sharing" the opinion. But all thinking individuals believe that there are real facts that all know and recognize because they "see" them; indeed, there are no differing opinions concerning the sun, the moon, and the stars, in the commonsense way in which their existence is understood. Similarly, there is agreement among people about existence, reality, truth, the reality of processes, connections, causes, and effects, which may serve as a measure of the correctness of an opinion. Or there is at least agreement about the conditions of correct thought and recognition to reveal, indicate, and prove the correctness of one opinion, which must be recognized as correct, or the opposite, through logical coercion. But we know that this agreement is shared only within strict limits; and even when there is agreement about certain sentences, they are interpreted differently, and words are most frequently used and understood in different ways.

[. . .]

23. (Permissible and Prohibited Expressions of Opinion). Although opinions cannot be suppressed, their expression and dissemination may be checked. The pragmatic statesman recognizes quickly that thoughts, including opinions and beliefs, cannot be forced on people, although one can strongly influence, check, or support them. In this context thoughts are "free" ("thoughts are duty-free"). But the expression of thoughts and views—and especially their public, that is, their consciously planned dissemination (propaganda, agitation)—is a free act that one can successfully order or prevent. More specifically, the negative approach, prohibition, is

the most convenient protection against imagined or real damages. And, truthfully, a publicly expressed opinion is different from an opinion expressed among friends or kept to oneself. The former wants to impress, be recognized and applauded, succeed, and be validated. Such an opinion is a weapon that can be employed with more or less talent and success. Even though the opinion itself is understood as purely intellectual—and remains that way as long as it is communicated among experts, colleagues, and class representatives—it is always based on ideology, a certain way of thinking, striving, and wanting that emerges from it and begs for participation, even solidarity in the struggle. This may be welcome or unwelcome, liked or hated by some, who are rarely noncommittal; if it is not the "right," accepted, positive opinion, it may be tolerated at best, that is, reluctantly, so that the representatives of the wrong opinion must suffer although one may not be able or willing to suppress them.

[. . .]

## COMMON OPINIONS, SECTION ONE. CONDITIONS OF A COMMON GROUND

1. (Possibilities of Correspondence). For two or more individuals to really share one "opinion" appears even more remarkable when it is less probable (A) under more difficult, entangled, and impenetrable conditions; (B) when individuals differ according to the conditions of their personal or social existence, needs, and interests; and (C) the more those individuals, who are capable and willing to make judgments, are different according to their talents, their way of thinking, and their emotional state, that is, the more everyone differs based on development and education. The opposite is self-evident. Dissent is more likely when these three complications converge and act together.

2. (The Problem of the Subject). An individual who understands a subject and is able to form an opinion about it normally, but not always, has a different "view" than a "layperson" (if this one has a view at all) and—again under normal circumstances—a more correct one. But the more difficult, entangled, and impenetrable a subject, the more often experts or equally intelligent and equally informed persons will make different judgments and harbor divergent opinions. An example are medical diagnoses. . . . Returning to the differentiation: harboring and forming an opinion is part of the organic will (*Wesenswille*), while its expression is possibly part of a divergent, even opposing rational will (*Kürwille*), which may also "form" an opinion. Thus, regarding a difficult question about which several individuals "agree," one may have formed an opinion and actually harbor the view, whose reasons he knows, while the others

merely express them by "religiously" repeating them. One follows and succumbs to the "authorities." One suppresses the disagreement, knowing that one is not qualified to pass judgment, or fearing disapproval or worse, not so much vis-à-vis an individual opinion, which may not generally be known, but when confronted with the unanimous and expressed opinion of many—however it arose. Silence suggests agreement, and one is counted among the audible voices of the choir. Each group, each circle forms a "public" opinion that appears internally and externally; this is commonly the opinion of authorities within each group or circle to which their members are subordinated. The more recognized the authority, the more prestige it gains, the more willingly, quickly, easily, and systematically conformity works. The transitions from mere repetition of words to repeating opinions are easy and frequent. Here too the law of perseverance operates: repeated opinions cling to authority that may no longer exist in the tight circle of "experts," or whose opinions on a specific subject are strongly attacked so that they have no real "value."

[. . .]

3. (Conditions of Existence). If the expectations are met, in a limited way, that experts are of one opinion concerning difficult questions, it follows even more so for easier questions that similar conditions of existence result in similar opinions, that is, the more the former diverge the more the latter will differ. . . . Everywhere common opinions emerge from a common existence, common estate, common class, and profession. Employment more than the place of residence, the way of making a living, but mostly property and freedom from a lack of both, are effective forces. Satisfaction with one's fate results in different opinions than dissatisfaction. Masters are more easily satisfied with the reigning order than servants. Secular leaders will represent the opinion that spiritual leaders are to be ranked second and that they assume too much—and vice versa. Rural inhabitants are normally of the opinion that they must be aware of being taken advantage of by city dwellers through fraudulence and dishonest talk, while urbanites find peasants rough and simple minded— and therefore in need of education—or clever and cunning, out for their own advantages, narrow-minded and closed to higher ideas. Thus, by and large it can be said that the same opinions are the expressions of the same interests and different opinions the expressions of different interests, which means that the struggle over opinions expresses mostly the struggle of estates and classes.

[. . .]

4. (Deeper Difference). But deeper and more general than these differences is—and it must be repeated here—the difference between ruling and ruled classes, between the high and the low, the rich and the poor, the educated and uneducated—even though these expressions for one and

the same difference may slightly differ and the formation of groups may slightly change. Accordingly, common and the same, or at least similar opinions, are formed here and there. This difference appears most frequently in religious garb.

[. . .]

5. (Differentiation). In addition, large numbers of people agree more easily upon an opinion than the educated ones because their views are typically split; the arrogance of knowing it better and the pleasure of disagreement are as significant as actually superior insight, competition of better knowledge, increased experience, and mature thought. These factors are more prevalent here than in a large group, which is determined more by basic feelings and corresponding opinions and is therefore more easily guided by them. . . . The differentiation of the individual may be recognized as an asocial factor: single-mindedness and the arrogance of knowing it better creates "loners" who are reluctant to be stereotyped. On the other hand, these characteristics—combined with actual superiority, external means, eloquence, and affability—are more suitable for a leadership role. Especially for the one who is convinced of his calling, who feels inspired and blessed by God, and who has the ambition to be celebrated and adored like a deity, or who labors under the illusion that he actually is one.

[. . .]

6. (Opinions and Expressions of Opinions). The fact that two or more individuals have the same opinion or "share one view" must be strictly separated from the fact that they express or represent the same opinion publicly. Naturally and in a crowd, the expression occurs "spontaneously": the individual has the urge and the need, under specific circumstances, to express his opinion, often however, in a small circle, that is, not publicly. The strongest incentive is listening to someone else's opinion or to that of many others when the need arises to applaud and agree or disagree and thereby to express a different opinion. By the way, the intensity of an opinion determines the wish to express it. The saying "when the heart is full, the mouth overflows" also applies to opinions. "I believe, therefore I talk." It becomes a duty to express a belief and to express it courageously and without timidity. . . . But the expression of an opinion may be separated from its natural context, it can be done with a specific intention, a specific purpose in mind, and without actually harboring the opinion. Its expression is conceived and thought of as an appropriate means to accomplish something because one knows or at least believes that this will work. The clearest example is the exchange, that is, buying and selling. . . . The expression of an opinion may be for sale and can be sold, or it can even be coerced. Other means by which an object can be obtained are also applicable here, such as persuasion, flattery, promises of future advantages, requests, threats, and orders. In every case it is about

initiating an expression of the real opinion, although the one who insists on it may be ambivalent about whether the expressed opinion is real or how real it actually is. . . . The sale of an expressed opinion as much as its use for personal gain is an exercise in personal freedom. The use for personal gain may also consciously involve the expression of one's own opinion: only the way of its expression, its tone and form, may suggest that this is done with a specific intent. But the offer and "sale" of one's own opinion converts the opinion directly into impersonal merchandise; like merchandise as merchandise belongs to no one but the arbitrary buyer, and like money, the most circulated merchandise, which has no owner but belongs to the one who earns it.

[. . .]

7. (Elections and Votes). Although the degree of difficulty of a subject may not allow everyone to harbor his own opinion, or to form an idea, it does not hinder anyone to express an opinion as his own, even when it is not arrived at personally. This is either because he really accepts it on the basis of someone else's authority—and someone he thinks is informed and able to judge—or he just expresses it for other reasons and purposes. The extreme case is its expression as an object of exchange, when it becomes marketable regardless of whether this or an opposite opinion is really harbored or adopted. This is very clear during elections and voting. The masses of ignorant people are driven like "cattle"—to express it roughly—to the "voting booth." Normally this is not even a difficult matter; at least it appears easy and simple to decide which party "is correct." Thought is directed by emotion, a very basic feeling, such as, here are the good ones, there are the bad ones, and one decides in favor of the good ones, even when what is good is consciously interpreted as in: for me, for my cause, and advantageous to my desires; bad is the opposite.

[. . .]

8. (Leadership). There is another occurrence: the more difficult a subject, the more similar the conditions of existence, and the larger the crowd, the more are the few—the leading and important individuals, regardless of whether they are informed as opposed to laypersons or not—in a position of expressing their opinion in ways that suggest that they speak for the masses. The reasons may be that (1) they submit to the opinion of the few, recognize the opinion through applause or at least silence, or that (2) the few, like advocates, lead the concerns of the masses by giving voice to their unarticulated feelings and needs and appear to speak for them, even when many feel and think differently, and finally that (3) emotions are stirred up among the masses by speeches and other means, even when those expressed thoughts and opinions are not understood. In all of these instances we encounter the leadership of opinion, which has strong and various meanings in social life. It exists although the leaders themselves

may say something else than they seem to mean or really mean. Even when the thus guided masses express an undetermined feeling, it is possible that a significant expression of opinion takes place that contains no truth except for the mood of the masses, filled with anger, hatred, and revenge, for instance, and aimed at destruction and defeat.

[. . .]

# 2

## Public Opinion

### SECTION ONE. PUBLIC NATURE

6. (Communication). Picture, speech, and writing, separately and collectively, act as means of communication. The audience, which is created by them, is not—like a theater audience—mostly gathered in a closed room (although a theater audience may also meet outdoors), except perhaps for the audience of a speech, for example, a religious congregation or a crowd at a political meeting. Each audience of this kind gathers, congregates, and constitutes an albeit weak unit that expresses its common moods, opinions, and wishes through signs of approval or disapproval, enthusiasm or aversion, and through quiet devotion or loud songs. The dispersed audience is different: it is often the unrelated and physically disconnected majority of audiences of the first kind, but more frequently it is the sheer number of individuals who are capable and somehow willing to receive and deal with the communication. Even the accidental audience is rarely strongly "mixed." It happens to understand and speak the same language and typically shares the same social background. For this reason, the mood is often uniform, for instance, at political meetings of the speaker's comrades, who invited him so that they could listen to what they wanted to hear; or measures have been taken to attract followers and reject the opponents and, if they voice their ideas, to silence them. There are often fights between invited and uninvited audiences. The gathered audience is typically noisy, whereas the dispersed audience of readers remains silent, although voices from the audience can be heard from among the "circle of readers."
    [. . .]

**9. (Struggles over Opinions).** As suggested earlier, it is the struggle that vitalizes the opinions of writers and speakers. The speech and the book, the pamphlet, and the newspaper article are weapons that are employed in the struggle of ideologies and ideas, as in the struggle of political ambitions and views.

These battles constantly change their substance. The struggles of the century, the decade, but mostly of the year, week, and the day, are characterized by the ardent participation of contemporaries. The spoken or written word ignites, speakers and writers express and disseminate their opinions, and there are helpers who "propagandize" their ideas, organize well-financed groups for "agitation" and "enlightenment," while a large audience embraces the received ideas. The battles of opinion move from objective differences as "differences of opinions" to personal animosity, the hostility of groups, ideologies, and parties, from words to deeds—from verbal to real injuries—and finally to organized fights with weapons, riots, and civil war. The expression of an opinion very frequently contains an insult for the one who thinks differently. His mind or character are questioned or even slandered, and often both are doubted. Opposite opinions are detested and called wicked. The dissident is a monster, and if he had once sympathized with those who judge him, he is now a "traitor."

[. . .]


## SECTION TWO. NEWS AND THE PUBLIC


**12. (Community and Tradition).** The conceptual difference between community and society corresponds to an internal difference of dominant communication and instruction.

Briefly stated, the "community" hands down preferably traditional opinions—beliefs and dogmas. The older generation is dedicated, first and foremost, to the education of the young. Fathers and mothers pass on experiences to their children, masters and teachers art and knowledge to their apprentices, followers, and students, who should acquire knowledge and practice for future generations. The upper class—and in particular the clergy—acts similarly as "teachers" toward people and laypersons; they provide those without a voice what is considered beneficial for them. The priest, historically the most important figure among teachers, is—according to his own belief or that of the people—in constant touch with heavenly powers. The latter circulate in the light on high or live on top of a mountain; they are ever present and yet exist and work effectively and in a special way through the bread and wine of Communion. The highest priest, in particular, who may be identical with the secular leader, knows the divine will and knows how to read it; therefore, he becomes a

Political news refers in its most extreme and upsetting version to war or peace and the dangers or opportunities regarding relations with other states, but also to internal upheavals, revolutions, and civil war, and—more recently—to consequential events, such as election campaigns, election results, constitutional battles, and legislation, all of which determine the welfare of families and individuals for decades to come.

In war there are victories and defeats, reasons for worries and reasons for hope, the potential of a continuation or the prospects for peace; in peacetime, there are the dangers of a disruption of peace that require constant attention, the relations between states and their citizens, that is, the many conditions of communication, including trade, which may lead to "trade wars" or to negotiations and treaties. In addition, internal matters are more present in peace than in war with news about laws and legislation, desired or rejected innovations, their probability and their expected, hoped for, or feared effects. These matters relate to the outcome of political elections, especially those involving the largest and most important legislative bodies, and to the "election campaign," which fosters speculations—hopes and fears—and promotes them as facts, raises curiosity and the need to know. Will the government win or will it be toppled? Is there a threat of radical change? Rebellion or civil war? Is property endangered? Will the poor have reasons to expect an improvement of their condition? Fear and hope are high, and excitement spreads with the news. Public speeches or addresses of statesmen and party leaders inside and outside legislative bodies—and meant for public information—draw attention or even cause a sensation.

15. (Business News). Business news is news about the condition of markets and business prospects; it focuses on the requested, offered, and paid price for all kinds of goods, monetary instruments and currencies, bonds and titles, that is, "stocks and shares" of all kinds. Their trade occurs in a specific place, "the stock market," which is important and known worldwide as the "stock exchange." These market and stock market reports do not cater to pure curiosity or intellectual interests, but are of strictly material interest to those winning or losing in the market and constitute the reason for trading—buying or selling. This interest, however, raises and intensifies participation in political affairs, which constantly affect the markets and improve or reduce business prospects. They are like natural events—fine weather and storm—which are observed because of their effects on the harvest and other consequences for the movement of prices. At least large newspapers—which represent the nature of the press—carry these discussions in their business sections. But there is also a specialized business press, which is dedicated exclusively to serving special commercial interests.

16. (The Need for News). Who needs news, who are its customers? Political news serves most immediately the politician, commercial news the

merchant. Both are businessmen with shared concerns related to avoiding damages and seeking advantages, whose object of attention is bound up with their personal welfare, benefit, and honor. For the politician it is the state, for the merchant his company; while the former depends more on honor the latter on benefits. But their business problems frequently meet. The financial needs and shortages of the state are often foremost on the mind of statesmen, especially when they involve foreign affairs and questions of power, namely, the use of power during wartime. The state needs a bank to receive and produce money, that is, the statesman needs the contact with "high finance," with merchants, who have incredibly large means at their disposal, either in cash or in their ability to collect and assimilate such means.

Earlier—and even nowadays in oriental states—taxes were raised by financial experts who had gained the right from the state in return for a predetermined payment ("a rent"). On the other hand, the affairs of the state are extremely important for the merchant—and not only when he is or wants to be in business with the state or when financial transactions or other deliveries of war goods during peacetime (but more so during war) suggest extraordinary profits. Not only their own state but also hostile countries are customers for defense- or war-related materials and machinery during peacetime, and they (normally) pay well. The domestic policies of trade, communication, and soon commerce in general, as well as foreign policies, are of extreme importance for many other goods, and especially for those of great value. They involve the merchant who sells but also the one who produces, and both in their eagerness to realize profits.

17. (Distribution). Before newspapers existed, statesman and merchant relied on news that they received through messengers or (more frequently) letters; the latter contained private and often secret news. This type of news system has not lost its importance or meaning. A public system of news has prospered alongside the private one, almost overshadowing its existence. The newspaper not only supplements private, state, or business news but serves to disseminate the news that is either intended for the public or escaped the desire for secrecy after—at least within the upper class—anyone has become an (amateur) statesman or businessman. The newspaper also serves the publication of news whose distribution is in the interest of bureaucratic institutions or individuals, and it becomes an organ for communicating supply and demand, a printed marketplace, especially for commerce, trade, and occasional sales, as well as for the exchange of uses and services.

Sombart (1902, 2:362) differentiates between individual and collective transmission of news—he could have called them private and public, when he applies the term "news publication." Completely different (also in Sombart's presentation) is the public service offered by the post office

# 3

## Public Opinion and "the" Public Opinion

### SECTION ONE. CREATION AND CHARACTER OF PUBLIC OPINION

**1. (Use and Concepts).** We should first disregard "a" public opinion. It is more desirable, instead, to differentiate clearly and sharply between public opinion and "the" Public Opinion.* The former is an external entity of multifarious, contradictory opinions, which are publicly voiced, and the latter a uniformly effective power. We have frequently suggested the following contradiction: "opining" means either thinking—in the sense of harboring a judgment, an intention, or a point of view—or is a shortened expression for articulating or announcing an opinion (a judgment, an intention, a point of view), used either among close associates, at a private function, or publicly in an open and generally accessible meeting with people. In the use of language, public opinion means not only the expressed opinion, but the one expressed explicitly for the public sphere, an audience, or the general public. But this meaning is mixed with the other one in ordinary language, when the general public, or the "audience," is

---

*Tönnies introduces three different meanings of public opinion, which are crucial for his theory and differ only in their objective meanings. They are mostly about differentiating among pure, applied, and empirical understandings of public opinion. (He uses definite, indefinite, and no articles, e.g., *die Öffentliche Meinung, eine öffentliche Meinung,* and *öffentliche Meinung.*) These terms are regularly translated into English as (the) "Public Opinion" and "(a) public opinion." He also uses *die öffentliche Meinung* and *eine Öffentliche Meinung* without specifying differences in their meanings. By marking essential semantic differences only by using upper or lower case initials, the differentiation is obvious only in writing.

133

also considered a subject of opinions. In this sense, there has been talk about opinions and the common property of the political public.

Scientific thought must not only separate these meanings but develop two different concepts—as it is done here—when we describe an "unarticulated" public opinion separately from "the" articulated (real) Public Opinion. In either case, the public demonstration and references to public, mostly political subjects, remain essential for both concepts. In the former case—concerning public opinion—the general public is implicated insofar as "all" individuals participate somehow actively or passively in public pronouncements of opinions. Here, however, for "the" Public Opinion, the subject is an essential, politically united public, in particular, which has agreed to opine and judge in a particular way and therefore belongs naturally to the public and public life.

This suggests a sharp contrast in the meaning of opining, which appears either mainly as an (intellectual) meaning of cognition or mainly as a (voluntary) meaning of an expressed will. One finds either publicly announced and widely shared views—manifold, colorful, and contradictory, even passionately struggling views—reflecting wishes, endeavors, and the interests of groups and individuals—subconsciously, consciously, and overconsciously; they are views that are also regularly judgments, negations, and approvals. Or, Public Opinion is essentially a will expressed in and through a judgment as a cohesive act and therefore is a conscious and expressed form of the will in the manner of a judicial order or judgment by any other decision-making body. It is an agreed-upon decision—the expression of the will of a totality that is not gathered as an audience or a subject of Public Opinion, except in spirit, and is typically too large to be represented as a gathering (1).

2. (The Analogy of the Assembly). There are, indeed, connections and transitions between one or the other meaning of "public opinion." Even an assembly, which is quite possibly entitled to pass laws for the whole state—or claims such a right—differs at the point of decision and in a state of deliberation.

In the first instance, it stands united in its entirety behind the decision because (typically) the will of the majority of those present—or at least a certain number (of those eligible)—counts as the will of the assembly and as such often also as the will of the whole. The latter is "represented" by the assembly and, as a people united in a state, supports the ideal assembly (e.g., the *Reichstag* or regional parliament), which is manifested in the real assembly.

In the second instance, the real assembly is split and torn apart by opposing opinions and speeches during its deliberations. The ideal assembly and the supporting whole of the people wait, so to speak, for the vote and the decision of the real assembly. Until then, the object, the bill, or the request is being "discussed" (the Latin expression for tearing apart) in a "debate," that is, in a fight or struggle of words, with gestures, applause or sounds of disapproval, and even violence.

The decision constitutes a kind of peace treaty, which, like other peace treaties, emerges from a decisive victory of one side (or one opinion); but often it is the result of giving way mutually—reaching a "compromise"— on views and intentions that would otherwise want to exclude or destroy the other side. It is possible that a unified majority agrees to a partial withdrawal in order not to offend or suppress a minority and to be comforting rather than provocative; it is equally possible that a majority, in a specific matter, can only be gained through a general retreat of different groups of opinions, which are otherwise capable of overcoming the resistance of a minority. Normally these groups may empathize with or show an affinity toward each other; at other times, as in grand politics, however, common opposition and hostility will make allies of the most heterogeneous and hostile groups. Individuals involved in deliberation and decision making are not necessarily and always the same; some participate in the deliberation but not in the decision or abstain from a vote; sometimes individuals have the right to deliberate but not the right to "act," that is, they have an advisory rather than a deciding voice.

To explain their mutual relationship one may, therefore, compare public opinion and "the" Public Opinion to an assembly. To reduce both ideas to a common denominator is a valuable conceptual exercise. There is no awareness of such a difference in the use of language. However, in reality public opinion is spoken about as a material object (I compare it to a vessel or mixing bowl) into which many different and incompatible ingredients are poured to start, more or less, a process of fermentation. Public Opinion, on the other hand, appears (in the other sense) as an intelligent being and unified power, often praised for its mysterious, lofty, and almost mythical nature, or accused and berated by those who feel mistreated by this deity.

Although we use the analogy of a deliberative voting assembly, we remain aware of the differences among many assemblies capable of deliberation and voting. I differentiate between natural and ordered assemblies, unorganized and organized ones, self-organized and externally organized ones, or already organized and gathering ones, as well as ideal and real assemblies (see above).

An ideal assembly refers to a corporate body insofar as it is a form determined by a collective will, either as an independent entity or as an organ of a general will or organization. The ideal assembly can be thought of as either a temporary and limited, or timeless and unlimited institution. A real assembly, representing a conceptual assembly or not, takes up a specific space and time; it has a material existence even when it must appear as a unit and therefore develops or wants to develop a common will. Normally one distinguishes an internal and mental state from its external and observable existence based on the latter's formal "opening" and "closing." Any assembly can meet under open skies, but even then its members are recognizable as such either by their lively actions or their manner of listening. In any case, those who are entitled to participate may wear signs or insignia; in the case of legally entitled members of a conceptual assembly they will have to prove their entitlement. Such meetings often occur behind closed doors—they are frequently secret and closed to the public. Public opinion lacks a specific space and time. It spreads like a fog, is completely unnatural, and is perceptible only through thought. It is a characteristic shared with the ideal assembly, but, as in a real assembly, many of those present will speak. Thus it resembles a deliberative assembly in which a noticeable mixture of voices, commotion, and shouts suggests the absence of a presiding officer, who—in an organized council meeting, for instance—will limit squabbles, censure certain expressions, and refuse the podium to an insolent speaker.

But even public opinion—conceptualized as an assembly—exists not quite without rules of order; certain rules of conduct are to be observed, according to an unspoken agreement, and the one who does not observe these conventional rules becomes "impossible" in society and is expelled morally, not unlike the dismissal of a member from a parliamentary assembly.

3. (Limits of Reception). The public of public opinion is actually unlimited. Whoever takes the floor may be heard around the world, sometimes literally, but not likely by all people (not even all adults).

Normally reception is limited by (1) the language one speaks, (2) the political arena in which the topic of a "speech" is meaningful and applicable, (3) the education of listeners or readers who can understand and contemplate what they hear, and (4) the power of the intellectual and moral "voice." The latter is influenced by (a) the internal or external reputation of the "speaker," (b) the weight of his arguments, his elegance and skillfulness in the use of slogans, amusing phrases and jokes, rhetorical figures, interesting and sensational news, and other means of provoking and stimulating attention, (c) the passion, pathos, and "tone of utter conviction" to "grab" his listeners or readers, and (d) the energy and ruthlessness with which he applies repetition, the most effective rhetorical device.

In addition, reception is also considerably limited by (5) already existing followers, for example, members of religious, party, or professional organizations, and often membership in a certain clique, group, or wing inside such organizations; in other words, by reputation and other impulses that determine the weight of a voice, especially in such a small circle. This also includes, above all, a recognized leadership role, as well as the glory of a celebrated name, the prestige of respected and generally desirable accomplishments, and success. This fact asserts itself irresistibly in small and large organizations—it has been described recently by Max Weber as *charisma*.

Finally, reception is limited by (6) external ways and means of dissemination, that is, by the way a book is marketed, the power of capital, and the connections and activities of a publisher, and especially by the type and size of the reading public of a periodical (magazine or newspaper) or its knowledge of how to acquire one. Such a degree of publicness depends in large part on numbers, spending power, willingness to sacrifice, and other characteristics of the members of a party or other groups. Still other characteristics contribute to an expansion of the public; for instance, the more important a newspaper, the more widely it is read and considered outside party circles.

4. **(The Press)**. The publication of books is (among the conditions of contemporary existence) not the most important means for making people heard, understood, and respected through public opinion. It is especially the periodical press—and as such the daily newspaper—which is generally called, and deserves to be called, "the" organ of public opinion. On the other hand, it is a major mistake to describe the press, therefore, as an organ of Public Opinion, or as being identical with it, and then suggest that it "makes" Public Opinion. The latter expresses the opposite of being its "organ" and is a typical case of misunderstanding, which often arises from a thoughtless submission to language.

Löbl deals with the "widespread but unjustified identification of the press with public opinion" (1903, 252). He reports the above interpretation without realizing its difference and offers the sentence that Public Opinion is the product of two factors: one is the original, living idea, the other, however, the "multiplying amplifier," represented regularly, although not without exception, by the press. Public opinion could develop and rise to power outside or opposite the press. "The propagator of the idea has other means of distribution and amplification at his disposal: the book, the parliamentary forum, organizational life, gatherings, public lectures, social events, direct agitation from person to person. All of these means have been successfully used in those cases in which public opinion was created without or even against the entire press" (Löbl 1903, 255). Löbl ignores the consequences of his differentiation between "the" Public Opinion and manifold public opinions, which he discovered long before me. To justify them, a more substantive understanding of Public Opinion must be introduced at this point.

5. **(Aggregate States of Public Opinion)**. There are differences to be made among various aggregate states of individual opinion and social, general, or Public Opinion. The degree of their firmness is the degree of their unity. But even in an air-like condition it may appear as a whole if

this condition arises after the evaporation of a firm and coherent mass, that is, from a liquid or an immediate solid state.

The firm Public Opinion flows when movement is introduced, which may happen through recognition, thoughts, or experiences that seize the general public—represented by us as subjects of Public Opinion. The firm Public Opinion is a general, unshakable conviction of the public, representing—as the holder of such convictions—a people or an even larger circle of "civilized humankind." For instance, there are a few such convictions in politics: that absolutism or autocracy are evil forms of government or, in law, that torture as evidence and the qualified death sentence are to be condemned as "barbaric."

Convictions can be in a state of flux, for instance, when it becomes known that an autocracy—whose overthrow Public Opinion registered with pleasure—is resurrected with violence and horror under the guise of constitutionalism, as in Russia under Stolypin. In this case, conviction gains through passion but loses firmness and wholeness; the view that this is a case of pseudoconstitutionalism and an unfair persecution of revolutionaries may be questioned, but it gains in intensity through opposition.

The unity of Public Opinion is most perfect concerning general ideas, expressed already in the emotion of language itself; it effects words like "tyranny," "despotism," "barbarism," sometimes also, "Middle Ages," among others, but is different when questions are raised, such as, Is this tyranny or are these medieval conditions? And it is completely different when something appears reprehensible or damnable and is so represented without following such a pattern. But in these cases a hazelike Public Opinion arises, derived from the liquid one or, with its help, from the firm one. This haze constitutes what is commonly known as "the" Public Opinion because it appears here in its most obvious, violent, and passionate form. At the same time it reveals its partisan character. Public Opinion is based on modern thought, whose general principles are shared by all parties and are rarely disputed; diverging opinions exist, however, not only in details but also in complete groups and parties headed by highly educated men and women. They depend on old views and representations, even though their voices may be normally drowned out, because the new, modern, and enlightened thought is also the more forceful one and has often irresistible power in the public sphere. Public Opinion always appears with the claim of being definitive, demands approval, and at least makes keeping silent—refraining from contradiction—a duty, with more or less success. The more perfect the success, the more it proves itself as "the" Public Opinion, despite the more or less silenced opposition.

The clearest example is provided by questions of religion. For instance, theocracy and the belief that a king will gain divine magic through being anointed have been all but abandoned in Europe. Undoubtedly, in every

gressively in the daily press. Public opinion, understood this way, is like a battlefield; even so, the struggle leads only occasionally—and in romance countries more frequently—to scuffles, duels, or murder plots. The audience and readers, particularly, act as onlookers in the struggle of opinions. But they are located in bad seats and can see only part of the stage—their side—as the right hemisphere of the brain belongs to the left eye and the left one to the right eye. Nevertheless, the reader of pamphlets and newspapers participates in the struggles, which are represented one-sidedly or in the way of his party representation and appear as the correct, and therefore as the victorious, ones.

The embattled idea becomes easily and frequently the publicly represented opinion because it is the correct one and the one accepted and recommended by decent and righteous people. It is shared at least by all reasonable individuals, friends of the fatherland, well-meaning and smart people, and this understanding merges into the idea of "the" Public Opinion. Sometimes it actually happens that a stated opinion about an item of public interest in an important and thoughtful newspaper is the best reasoned, the most sensible, and—in terms of good taste and correct feelings—the most guaranteed opinion. It happens more often, however, that apparent reason, dominating thought, or faddish taste meet feelings that support the suggestions of the day. One way or the other, it can already be or become the general, "the" Public Opinion. But this hardly happens on account of a publicized opinion in one journal. There has to be agreement among several, and they must exceed the boundaries of party ideology so that opposition newspapers fear to offend their readers and are forced to issue a skillfully hidden retraction or significantly reduce their counteropinion.

This is the "stream" of Public Opinion that breaks all resistance; it can be tremendously reinforced by important newspapers—even one of them—which cannot be ignored. Normally this stream already exists and the press—a weekly, even monthly journal—creates a wind that is capable of stirring up the calm waters, like Aeolus, who releases the wind from his bag. It may be a moral, political, or aesthetic wind—which must howl whether there is a reason for it or not. More often, however, a strong wind of Public Opinion rises—caused by a special event, a "scandal," or a "case"—without the cooperation of the newspapers, which merely mediate the news (and can get to an audience in different ways). Naturally such a wind will reach publishers and writers of newspapers, but if it is an adverse wind, they will only reluctantly join its direction; this means that an opinion carried by the wind opposes their own principles and ideas or those of their party. They will rarely risk walking into the wind, which may topple them. Instead, they prefer walking with the wind, slowly and reluctantly, although a storm can break their resistance, making them feel driven involuntarily.

## THIRD SECTION. VULGAR APPEARANCE
## OF "THE" PUBLIC OPINION

**17. (Public Opinion and the Newspaper Business).** The permanent object of observation and discussion is the public opinion of the day, which does not differentiate between public opinion or "the" Public Opinion. Very frequently there is talk about a split public opinion, as if its unity would be the normal rule—which is actually true of the articulated Public Opinion. English public communication refers customarily to large "bodies" and "sections" of public opinion, while it understands by *Public Opinion* absolutely "the" Public Opinion, although important writers recently added an article or the words, "as a whole" (3).

Although it is not an essential characteristic of those manifold and intricate voices of the day to be represented by contemporary writers, it has become a significant phenomenon of the era. And it may be just as well their normal characteristic to represent opinions, viewpoints, feelings, and endeavors of parties, be they organized or unorganized, large or small, chiming in (just this once) or (which is the rule) fighting each other more or less vehemently. When writers—journalists—share the views and feelings they express, their task is undoubtedly easier and this is so often—perhaps in most cases. It is also not so rare that a belief will emerge, or at least be reinforced and grow, through the act of expression itself. But obviously this kind of correspondence is not necessary: the paid writer follows, like all mercenaries, the flag whose bearer feeds him and promises booty; he can do what he must do, and if he had a view or "conviction," it would shrink and die for a lack of food. Experience will reveal that it is easier for him to express a specific—and dictated—view when his own view is less formed; he does not need it for himself but exclusively for others, externally, and in the service of his "superiors."

There is a consensus among those who have lately written about the press that the newspaper, and particularly the large one, is and has become a capitalistic enterprise whose immediate purpose is to extract profits from the business. Consequently, writers have to follow this purpose and conform—they must express or conceal whatever promotes or prevents profits, respectively.

The idea of the interest of the newspaper guides the "spirit" of its expressions. These interests are essentially limited by the approval or disapproval of (a) readers, (b) subscribers, and (c) advertisers. Readership normally includes subscribers and advertisers; anything outside these sponsors has meaning for them largely for purposes of their own fulfillment and growth; and besides, the extent of the readership increases name and reputation of the newspaper. The size of its "circulation" is such an indication, and it is based partly on sales on the open market—single sales—and partly (in Germany, at least for the most part) on subscriptions. The majority of the latter belong to party members who wish to have their specific views and ideologies represented by the newspaper they read, subscribe to, and generally support; they read "their" newspaper with satisfaction, when such opinions are expressed openly and strongly, but they are outraged when an "article" is indecisive, is not "ideological enough," or even agrees with an opposing viewpoint. Even advertisers are preferably, but not exclusively, supporters of opinions represented by the newspaper; some of them back the newspaper consciously through advertisements because they want to support a good cause. Such an intent sometimes goes beyond the purpose of introducing their company or their products; the indirect effect—which benefits the business—is as important as the immediate one. Concerning the newspaper business, however—and the experts agree—advertisements mean more than subscriptions; consequently, advertisers must be shown more consideration than subscribers when pure business interests are at stake. The interests of the businessman are more important than those of the party member. They will assert themselves negatively: the rage over immediate or indirect material damage will be more vehement and expressed more strongly than dissatisfaction with an ideological wrong, an aberration, or a "derailment." The manager of a newspaper acts poorly— according to the publisher's judgment and that of others behind newspaper capital—when an important "large" client withdraws his advertisements from the newspaper.

At the same time, advertisers are not satisfied with announcements or recommendations on the back page of the newspaper; advertisements up front, on the "forehead" or "chest," so to speak, are more precious, also those placed across or amid a thoughtful political discourse or fictional account. But the public notices such an intent and notices the voice of the charlatan. Parts of the public—those who have been "burned"—are suspicious and shy away from the fire. Sales are better served by an apparently uninterested recommendation, like the recommendation by a writer who is obviously convinced of the value, or an obvious, strictly objective editorial judgment. Such opinions can be named ("cited"), they can also be more or less genuine and innocent, like—undoubtedly—opinions about books and other goods, which a publisher or merchant will use to his advantage. However, opinions meet these purposes also as much when they are ordered, that is, invented or falsified.

Even more effective are opinions that are apparently not advertised or paid for but emanate exclusively and immediately from the desk of a writer or an editor. Especially when the reader receives them with the same trust with which he consumes the daily editorial. Therefore, it is a task to deceive the reader and one that can be carried out in many ways.

The simplest method is that of the hidden advertisement; the process of hiding can be more or less complete. Contrary to other cases of a moral life, shamelessness grows with the completeness of the disguise. Observers agree that French newspapers use hidden advertisements intentionally and regularly. It is nowhere unknown. If it is recognizable despite the disguise, it takes on cunning forms: it escapes from the main part of the newspaper and the business section to "below the line" [the feuilleton or feature section—Trans.], where the "occasional" mention of a car tire, for instance, can be placed "unobtrusively" in an exciting novel or in a funny (or what is supposed to be funny) feature article.

The business section is, by the way, most frequently exposed to the alien element of such commercial interests. Those who know the secret maintain that the large German newspapers are "especially in their business section absolutely incorruptible" (Feldhaus 1922, 38). Among the French press corruption is an obvious fact; the business section is "simply sold to the highest bidding bank house" and the public is at the mercy of the business practices of some company that wants to make money. Yes, public opinion in France approves of it (Feldhaus 1922, 38). The French newspaper does not live, as do those in most other countries, directly off its advertisers; the customer-reader rejects the purchase of packets of commercial inserts and leaves it to commercial companies to introduce their products without his help. Instead, there are more hidden advertisements, for instance, the short announcement smuggled into the text of the newspaper is a specialty of French business, which knows how to recommend itself in a less imposing manner, which must appear more charming to the French.

18. (Corruption). Like all characteristic phenomena of modern life, the daily press demonstrates its sharpest and freest features in the colonized states, that is, most remarkably in the largest and most important one, the United States of America. The "corruption" of the press is only a striking sign of the corruption of public life as such. The literature of the country—which, to a large extent, is nothing but a bound collection of newspaper clippings, a "magazine," that is, a cultural warehouse—nevertheless may be credited with containing voices that expose the growth of corruption; they dare talk about the press "like it is." The fact that it is first and foremost a business does not distinguish it any longer from the European press. Dr. Robert Brunhuber, a journalist, suggests that the dangers of capitalistic newspaper companies—once proclaimed by men like Lasalle—have been recognized and accepted today by people who stand on the grounds of a capitalistic order. He mentions, as evidence, a remark by Theodor Barth, "the idea of affecting the public ideologically disappears behind the question: how can the sale of printed paper bring maximum profits?" (Brunhuber 1908, 30). This form of newspaper capitalism devel-

221–262); in its relation to public opinion he states that the pamphlet contains collective ideas only insofar as the author of such a publication shares the opinions and leanings that rose to power in his environment. Only a comparison of all simultaneously published materials of this kind could lead to the pamphlet or brochure becoming a source of insights about public opinion. "Results will only come from examining which ideas are repeated most frequently, where they connect with older ones, and how they lead to new ones. In each case it is important to also trace evidence of the distribution of each pamphlet." But even this is misleading. "Educated" circles—separated by knowledge and similar economic conditions—form opinions and prejudices that "are perhaps only held and shared by a minority but create the impression of being shared by all, since the majority, which lacks the means of expression (and this also goes for other minorities), has no access or is incapable of making itself heard."

His remarks turn to the press (chapter 7) and the historical development of its three characteristics: publicity, periodicity, and topicality. In what relation does the newspaper stand to public opinion? There are differences among the newspaper, the party paper, and the political press; the latter is partial itself. The press is affected by public opinion and forms it. Economic conditions force publishers (1) to consider the disposition of their readers and advertisers and (2) to submit to the mechanism of big business organizations. The journalist must balance the interests of the owner and the party or the government and look out for the public at the same time. There are certain analogies between the press and public opinion, but there is no parity. The effect and importance of the newspaper reached a certain peak already during the seventeenth century. But only the French Revolution brought about real domination by the press, which increased successively during the nineteenth century, especially after the installation of press freedom. Now the press is free, but not its journalists on whose shoulders rests the official party yoke (Brunhuber's expression). Also business ties with their considerations and connections impose heavy constraints on press freedom. The wholesale organization of the news flow, especially through news agencies, results in the uniformity of newspaper content. In special cases, freedom of opinions is more restricted than ever; the narrow interests of parties and professional organizations, the lack of education, and the apathy regarding public matters also reduce the effectiveness of the press. Its real weakness, which is also its strength, rests on its origins in an urban culture, especially its metropolitan character. There is also "a public opinion that is built on traditions with roots in feelings rather than in hastily exchanged inspirations at the news market" (1914, 303). The former fights newspaper influence and is especially strong among the rural population, where the press plays an insignificant role.

The press has a special task as mediator between people and government. People see in the principle of the public sphere the safest guarantee of civil liberties. But the newspaper does not represent all of public opinion and cannot influence it totally. An appalling weapon is "killing with silence," aimed at the appearance of political personalities or used against serious scientific or artistic works. The beginnings of news trusts for the dissemination of opinions makes progress, and soon "free spirits" are those who attempt an escape from the opinion monopoly of the press.

Finally Bauer examines "action" as a means of expressing public opinion (chapter 8), especially politics and its most terrible and splendid phenomenon—war. There is a reverse relationship between war and public communication; war is the death of the hollow phrase. But public opinion affects war strongly, and war affects public opinion. The same relations exist between action and opinion. Professional politicians are the journalists of action: they do not ask for the real value of their propositions and requests, but they turn their eyes only to the public opinion of the moment. Thus personal and political aspects are introduced into the law and, even worse, into internal administration or even the administration of justice. Wherever the "rational part of public opinion" begins to dominate, it shows almost consistently the negative effects of its nature, which makes for progress. Morally stronger authorities resist. But most important is the struggle of the active individual against public opinion, which must follow him sooner or later, especially if he is an important statesman (5).

22. (Additions). I report this extract from Bauer's writings because I appreciate this chapter as a preliminary work and recommend it to those who want to study the nature of public opinion. I think I have provided sounder reasons for several of its ideas through my differentiation of (1) the states of public opinion (and opinion generally) and (2) public opinion and "the" Public Opinion. In addition, I would like to add the following remarks.

1. Bauer himself has pointed out that he passed over the "fine arts" as means of expressing public opinion. In truth, all public communication, and particularly its more primitive and most circulated type, is unthinkable without "illustration." Since the picture is older than the letters that are derived from it, it keeps its attraction for the world of readers, especially women and youngsters who like to look rather than think. The woodcut and the engraving, formerly restricted to monthly and weekly magazines and capable of multiple mechanical reproduction, have invaded the daily newspapers, which must now use colored prints to maintain their position. While religious representations of the "divine story" or stories of saints, as well as sagas and fairy tales for children, always appear new and fresh, the senses of the modern individual demand from a picture the significant, the new, the interesting, and, if possible, the "piquant."

Whatever occupies public opinion, it also wants to see and quickly, too, before it thinks of something else. The less important is committed to memory and glorified in monuments: people and objects of the past appear effectively as being in the present, and respect for them becomes more and more conventional and is dealt with like a business. The typical modern individual who participates in public opinion does not want to deal with it all the time. Also, the characteristic movement, "L'art pour l'art," refuses to put art in the service of life, religion, or other social contexts, but wants to make it the object of pure play, indulgence, and curiosity.

A. I want to discuss also the formation of an organization as an important means of expressing public opinion—especially in political matters. The latter attracts a collective "holding of opinions" and more so when it realizes itself as a wish or desire. An organization means connected power, joint means, especially money, and a common account based on uniform and orderly rules. Organizations for political purposes, especially, are expressions of public opinion; even secret societies and conspiracies are included as long as they want to be and should express a common idea or endeavor. Organizations may operate fervently in the open or in secret on the dissemination of a specific idea. There is talk, consideration, and decision making in organizations, which may request and use the right to punish members. Discipline increases its power and fortifies its structure. Interestingly enough, a competent leader may operate like a field marshal (and is called general) in religious societies, for example, the Jesuits and the Salvation Army. Like the Society of Jesus earlier in the Roman Catholic religion and its church, Freemasons and their descendants, the Illuminati and others, influenced public opinion in later centuries. The "club" had a significant and immediate political meaning in England, which was transplanted to France immediately before the great revolution. In these clubs people "spoke loud and without restraint about human rights, the advantages of freedom, and the great abuses of different conditions of life" (Buckle, 378). The club of the Jacobines gained most powerful political significance, which, according to Aulard, became translator as much as leader of public opinion (Buckle, 125). In romance countries freemasonry has gained significance as an expression of liberalism—and recently also increasingly as an expression of pronounced anti-German feelings in the nineteenth and twentieth centuries. G. Maier (*Ethische Umschau*, June 1915) thinks that the political activity of the order in Italy had led widely to a misunderstanding of its tendency; leadership in war politics by the lodges is the first example of a planned influence on public opinion, as it had earlier come from France and Bonapartism.

This is just a reminder of the general meaning of organizations in contemporary politics; they regularly effect destruction and occasionally the unification of thoughts and desires.

Therefore, organizations are an essential part of social thought and will power as well as the basis for their expression, which one calls either public judgment or public opinion, public conscience or something similar. The fact that these judgments and opinions express themselves very frequently with a peculiar certainty and have become more objective while losing their naivete—according to different interests—must be credited partly to organizations and their concern about the ideological. (Klein, 177).

B. An organization meets periodically and can—for its own purpose—call meetings that are aimed at increasing membership and its means, or are deemed suitable for representing general or specific ideas of a program. Election meetings are of great significance in modern states, like party election organizations. They call themselves organizations and are a mechanization of the political will through party leaders, who are well described in America and England as "wire pullers."

Professional politicians work (in the United States) under the leadership of managers and wire pullers, with such an ensemble and with such a complete indifference or unconsciousness concerning good or evil that they evoke the image of an automatic, blindly functioning mechanism of a machine. Such was the effect that the expression "machine of the organization" became a nickname that has lasted until today and is preferred to "caucus" (Ostrogorski 1912, 365).

The public gathering, which gains a politically more significant meaning as an election meeting (in America: primary), gives the impression of a single will when it expresses its voice and opinion through applause for a speaker or through other means. It runs a stormier or quieter course, and it is not true that commotion is its permanent characteristic. Public opinion can express itself in such a meeting with or without noise, but more likely as a common idea, a common judgment, when speech follows speech and is heard with quiet but decisive approval.

C. There are other, direct forms of demonstrating immediately currents of opinions when a meeting with its decisions must demonstrate and prove the existence of a strong current of opinions and will. Thus the meeting wants a public showing and taking to the street or market is the simplest way for the many who want to demonstrate their conviction—because words are at first unnecessary. They express their wishes and opinions through natural means and forms, like flags and emblems and the singing of songs, but especially through participation in large numbers, which heightens the realization of power in all participants. Thus the holy march, the "procession," the raising of flags, or the ringing of bells become favorite forms of demonstration. They express the mood of the people and frequently their public opinion.

opinions by their wholesomeness or harmfulness and not by their internal values, their truth or probability. Therefore opinions are measured by the welfare of individuals and prescribed as means of reaching a specific goal in a common pursuit of a purpose, or of rejecting or dissuading other goals as impediments on the way to personal happiness, career, and competition. Effects depend directly only on expression, and this may happen by way of the rational will *(Kürwille)*, which denies a held opinion outright; however, expression affects thought, especially through frequent repetition, resulting in accommodation and balance; for instance, political opinions change like the nonbeliever who becomes religious through frequent sermons. The civil servant in a monarchy may hold republican views, reinforced substantially by education, social intercourse, and reading, which he must suppress for the sake of his career. Even more, he must appear now and then to embrace loyal, monarchistic sentiments; the more success, the more his antipathy diminishes and the sound structure of his "former" conviction softens and is finally reduced to mist and fog. A new organ slowly evolves through this process, and he gains a deeper appreciation of monarchistic ideas the more old "prejudices" fade away. This happens when someone repeats something so frequently (and, in the worst case, even lies) that he finally believes it. The social structure as a whole, as well as political or commercial businessmen in particular, are constantly compelled to engage in self-denials. The merchant demonstrates most directly how a purpose leads him to suppress or adapt his opinions. The public opinion of his profession demands shrewdness, first and foremost, and the success that comes with it. The same goes for the statesman and the public opinion of his colleagues, which is joined, in this case, by the real, civic Public Opinion, since the general interest in success and therefore cleverness is overwhelming.

Insofar as the Public Opinion preferably refers to political life, political leaders, and the law, it also makes judgments true to its purest nature, according to success; it acts, based on past or expected success, affirmatively or negatively, admiringly and glorifying, or in disgust and with disdain for people and events. Therefore it demands approval, especially when there is self-interest in its future success, based on the insight that such a success must be sought. War represents a strong and clear example when the whole nation is most interested in a victory, and consequently Public Opinion wants such a success. It becomes a duty for fellow citizens not only to participate in wanting this success (which needs little pressure) and hoping for it, but also to think and believe that it will happen, and to think of it not only as a possibility but as a sure and certain event. This means to not voice an opposing opinion because it is disadvantageous, discouraging, and upsetting for fellow citizens, and maybe even for soldiers. Such behavior is branded explicitly a fabrication when it is based on pure conviction and is the spontaneous expression of spontaneous feelings and thoughts: the accused are cited for discouragement and running down the cause as *défaitistes,* in French, as if they wished for and wanted to bring about a defeat. In truth, there is the suspicion that wishful thinking is the father of the idea or, if that does not make sense, the direct result. "He does not believe in victory because he does not want it" and "he does not wish for a victory because he does not believe in it." The word "because" in the second sentence signals an insight that not believing leads to not wishing. But is also easy to add a basic relationship, namely, that the sin of nonbelief results in the larger sin of cursing.

Real Public Opinion and religion both vilify a deviant opinion as a sin. Even though they are not interested in having a deviant opinion expressed or disseminated ("propagandized"), its assessment (i.e., its rejection) is based on having the opinion—it is the *materia pecans.* The judge assiduously traces such an opinion to ill will, stubbornness of the heart, and closing the mind to truth. This is especially so regarding the immediate goals of the Public Opinion of the day, or even fluid public opinion. It is different with objects that are the focus of a hardened Public Opinion. For instance, when the *Zeitgeist* requires thinking that torture is barbaric or the Inquisition is an infamous mark on humanity, it is initially inconceivable for a "modern" individual not to agree. Those who become defenders of such cruelties may want to reintroduce them and return to those times in which they could happen. What other reasons are there but self-interest, the interest of an estate or class, that wants to rule and suppress the free spirit or return its former rule? There is a mixture of expression and belief in the truth of such "nonsensical" and "disgusting" opinions that are contained in negating and damning judgments. Negation and damnation, agreed upon by the *Zeitgeist* (i.e., by a hardened Public Opinion), are based partly on emotion—an overwhelming feeling and strong conviction—and partly, however—and this is more characteristic of Public Opinion—consciously on suffocating those incorrect and pernicious opinions and suppressing them as a public menace. Emotion is especially characteristic of large crowds; superior consciousness, on the other hand, is the natural characteristic of leaders, who know that they are responsible for consequences and effects and who—as intellectuals—are more trained in thinking generally, like the experienced man and the master of any art or craft.

25. (Leaders of "the" Public Opinion). There are leaders of "the" Public Opinion, just as there are leaders of political parties. Sometimes they are the same, but only when the party is stronger, capable of accentuating a general feeling and desire, and carried along by triumphant propaganda. This only happens when the party is accommodated by the needs of the "time," the prevailing perceptions and experiences, and when formulas

and slogans are irresistible. At that point Public Opinion grows in its favor; Public Opinion itself takes sides. In this sense, there is an obvious fluctuation among large, powerful parties of an educated consciousness—conservative and changing, aristocratic and democratic, authoritarian and liberal—a rhythmic movement, like a pendulum. At the same time, a second string of alternatives—mutating democratic, liberal politics and ideology—continues to arise. This duality can be recognized in Europe and even in colonial countries.

In contrast to religion (even in opposition to it, according to some), Public Opinion has a scientific aura. There is a connection between its freer formation and the increasing influence of scientific thought. The observation of the latter, which provides us with the insights of Public Opinion, marks this era—the present in its broadest meaning, or "modernity"—decisively and clearly. Thus leaders of scientific thought, scientists as teachers, who are the natural and real leaders of Pubic Opinion, are of direct public importance, but even more so indirectly and according to the extent to which their thoughts, research, and teaching are relevant to questions of general consequence or public importance. These are either social questions, very closely tied to the problems of economic life, or questions of a political or moral and especially spiritual nature.

Throughout modernity, there are different leaders of public opinion within nations, who are described in the following.

A. Representatives of the traditional teaching profession, that is, the clergy, whose influence was overwhelming during the first half of this epoch and remains significant throughout the second half. Naturally their impact is closely related to, but not identical with, the continuing importance of religion for Public Opinion, especially with the rising prominence of a religious and theological laity. But during this time in modern societies, Public Opinion slipped more or less out from under the influence of religion and theology generally and therefore of the clergy. Moreover, it largely opposed these powers and—according to our applied conceptualization—actually became Public Opinion per se. The new teaching profession developed from the old one while creating more distance between them.

B. University teachers were at first closely related to and largely identical with the old profession. In intellectually backward countries like Spain and England (based on the state of their general science education), these teachers remain by and large members of the clergy, but with different effects. There are Roman Catholic and Anglican clergy, respectively (with occasional dissidents), with a correspondingly weaker or stronger share in the new sciences. Otherwise, the theological faculty provides the context, joined often by jurisprudence, the other dogmatic faculty; both represent the past, which is the traditional form of a valid truth. The new faculties, on the other hand, medicine and philosophy, are more or less filled with the spirit of the future; they want what is new and therefore explore existence quite thoroughly.

The influence of universities on the formation of Public Opinion in German-speaking areas, and especially of those two faculties that are codetermined by the natural sciences, has been vigorous indeed. It has been noted mostly in the Protestant part of Germany. The expression "enlightenment" *(Aufklärung)* is German and typical; the eighteenth century was named for it after humanism had already found its domain in German universities. The revival of the classics, especially the association with Greek ideals of humanity, predated the triumphs of the natural sciences; the latter would be tolerated and even supported in the spirit of the two older faculties. The natural sciences and a related, reform-minded philosophy were admitted to German universities earlier than elsewhere. The competition among noblemen and their self-interests in utilizing the new insights contributed significantly to it. The impact of English, French, and Italian universities on the formation of the modern Public Opinion is much less important; an existing or returning clerical influence predominated during the eighteenth century and even extended into the nineteenth century—at least in Great Britain—while the revolution in France repeatedly paralyzed and broke this influence.

C. Similarly, the rest of the teaching profession—except for university teachers—has been significantly effective, although generally less free and more under the rule of spiritual or secular authorities. Among them are especially high school—and later middle school *(Realschule)*—teachers; the former worked through conserving classic ideals, the latter through applying the natural sciences and modern languages. Only during the nineteenth century did primary school teachers gain in importance, especially in urban and metropolitan areas. They participated within Protestantism and in its spirit—but also for other modern ideas—in the dissemination of newer viewpoints and therefore Public Opinion, partly within the profession itself and partly within the larger field of their teachings. In addition, these teachers also maintained or occupied positions of enlightenment abandoned or barely defended by higher classes of teachers, as much as the insufficient protection of their social position or their inadequate equipment allowed.

D. However, when all teachers disseminate ideas and opinions directly and professionally through the living word, they are soon joined by other speakers and preachers, who excite and incite or relax and appease the people. They fight in the front line of the battle of opinions—among them free speakers rather than appointed or paid ones—and speak out mostly in favor of new, struggling, reforming, or even revolutionary opinions and ideas. Although formerly almost exclusively religious, or working the

And indestructible as are the stars.
and
We will be free, just as our fathers were,
And we will die before we'll live as slaves.

Undoubtedly, he contributed mightily to an appreciation of "liberty" and therefore to the rise of political and religious liberalism in the first part of the nineteenth century and beyond. And so did the general impression of his personality and his sympathetic idealism, which is a reminder of religious enthusiasm; this is an impression described by Goethe,

He shines before us like a comet, disappearing,
Uniting boundless light with his ingeniousness
[Er glänzt uns vor, wie ein Komet entschwindend,
Unendlich Licht mit seinem Licht verbindend]

which contributed to the transfiguration of Schiller's name, whose traces have still not disappeared.

Since leading Public Opinion is connected quite naturally to the means of expression, and since the rest of the arts, besides teaching, speech, writing, and poetry, belong to these means of expression, artists become, if not leaders, at least companions of Public Opinion. Primarily stage actors as translators of dramatic poetry, but also well-known and admired painters, sculptors, architects, and musicians, affect taste, pleasure, and thus indirectly opinions of what is beautiful. But since the beautiful and the good are constantly involved with each other, they affect not only aesthetic but also ethical Public Opinion, and finally also political Public Opinion. Thus the fine arts and their great representatives have participated since the Renaissance in the separation of an ascetic idealism from modern thoughts and life, or they were involved in what Heine and others had called the emancipation of the flesh. Even the art of construction appeared lighter, friendlier, even frivolous, during Rococo and stood in contrast to a serious, dark, and noble Gothic style. Moral seriousness, deepened by science and philosophy, recurs in the arts from time to time. Public Opinion submits itself to it by rewarding artists who prove themselves in grand style to be masters, who stir up a mood in the soul that is related to religious feelings. When an artist—of whatever kind—joins the educators of humankind, he adapts Public Opinion, or the spirit of the times, and enters into an exchange with these powers. The important artist—in harmony with the important thinker—will always affect Public Opinion of the century, while the less important artist or thinker often affects Public Opinion of the day in ways that are much more conspicuous, splendid, and intoxicating.

# 4

# "The" Public Opinion and Its Characteristics

## SECTION ONE. SOCIOLOGICAL CONTEXTS OF "THE" PUBLIC OPINION

**1. (Forms of Social Will).** I have formulated the concept of the Public Opinion so that it expresses a form of social will, that is, a societal will in contrast to all other forms of a communal will. Here is a summary of the theory of the forms of a social will that differentiates among six forms of communal and societal will respectively, of which three represent simple or elementary forms and three combined or advanced ones.

The following table contains these categories:

Table 3

| A. *Community* | B. *Society* |
|---|---|
| (a) understanding, (b) tradition, (c) faith | (d) contract, (e) norm, (f) doctrine |
| (aa) concord, (bb) custom, (cc) religion | (dd) convention, (ee) legislation, (ff) Public Opinion |

Forms identified by simple and double letters are the elementary and composite or advanced forms, respectively; the latter are also called forms of a collective will.

All of these forms are related, connected, and merge into each other. The A-forms are original and have become essential—they correspond to forms of an individual organic will *(Wesenswille)*. The B-forms are derived and made essential—they correspond to forms of an individual rational

177

will *(Kürwille)*. The A-forms of the social will are not necessarily expressions of an organic will, as B-forms are not necessarily expressions of a rational will. However, individual, organic will participates decisively in A-forms, and individual, rational will in B-forms of the social will. Also, these forms must be recognized and judged by themselves as communal and societal forms.

The principle of categories reflects the threefold nature of the human soul, which is based in a vegetative state, acts in an animalistic life, and completes itself as spirit in a mental and specifically human existence. This trinity must always be understood in terms of interaction or collective action.

Each of these forms connects human souls and wills by influencing individual practice and (directly or indirectly) thought in an initiating, compelling, and inspiring manner, that is, by influencing the will threefold. The A-forms are derived mostly from common feelings, the B-forms from common thoughts. B-forms are only the "rationalized" (or reflected) A-forms, which are connected to reason and purpose through human thought and are therefore always dependent on them and within their spheres. They are, so to speak, their imitations, re-creations, or substitute forms, which can gain power as constructs of human thought and are, in their external effects, much superior to the original forms. One like the other contains imperatives; but those of the B-forms are sharply limited, specifically "formulated," hard and rigidly formed, whereas those of the A-form are smooth, soft, justifiably unspecified, and vividly figurative. The transition at least from simple A-forms to simple B-forms may be compared to a process of paralysis. Thus tacit, loose understanding and communication become a formal agreement, a specific arrangement, a contract; a pleasing, thoughtful, and poetic tradition turns into tough regulation, and a pious, devoted, fantastic, and vivid faith results in dry doctrine or rigid norm. The expressed formula is finally firmed up—or fixed—in writing, set down in a document, and merged in a book. The document assumes its own dignity, a contract becomes sacred, and a book is elevated to "holy scripture." Rationality and logic enter the service of belief and imagination. One day, in one century, however, rationality will liberate itself from servitude to seek and find its own way.

2. (The Development of Forms of the Social Will). The development from a predominantly communal to a societal age is characterized preferably by the retreat or change of the higher A-forms into higher B-forms. This is the rationalization of the spirit, the progress from culture to civilization, and the prevalence of an urban, metropolitan coexistence with the rise of trade, technology, and science. We recognize differences and contrasts in these substantial processes and in every cross-section of historical development; they represent more or less of the old or new spirit, prefer-

A scientific conceptualization must observe religion in its liquid and air-like forms and Public Opinion in its various states and compare the firm forms of religion with those of Public Opinion, the liquid ones of the former with the liquid ones of the latter, and so on. All the while the direction of the development must be observed, whether the process moves in the direction of firmness or liquidity, because liquid forms exist before and after firm ones. When we state the liquid or air-like forms of a religion—resulting from its firm state—we do not pretend that the belief of individual followers is shaky or deteriorated, liquidized and disappeared because of doubts or critical doctrines, but we rather maintain that religion, as a will to believe changes, becomes soft and liquid, or disappears as steam or fog. Obviously, however, there is an interaction between these developments.

[. . .]

An air-like quality of religion can be noticed among people in the presence of "superstition," which is partly welcomed and supported by the real and official religion and partly regarded with indifference. Often, however, it is disputed and opposed, especially when it is part of a former, suppressed, and outdated religion. Nevertheless, superstition can be widespread, strong, and quite similar to religion, if not, on special occasions, even superior.

According to ordinary language use, religion becomes more similar to Public Opinion, the more religion reveals itself or is understood as an antidote to dominant thought against specific events or practices and, therefore, against individuals enthralled and affected by them. Also, Public Opinion becomes more similar to religion (in its predominant sense), the more the former appears and is recognized as an affirmed idea, a piece of *Weltanschauung*. A common and neutral concept may be Public Judgment, which is a nationally dominating, more or less determined, favorable or unfavorable, positive or negative opinion of people, events, deeds and misdeeds, laws and regulations, opinions and doctrines, real and possible "questions" concerning "divine" and "human" topics, that is, of the world as such or *Weltanschauung*.

Another neutral concept is the Imperative, the order to recognize and uphold as truth such imaginations, opinions, ideas, and doctrines and not to contradict, not to think differently, and not to express different ideas. Every will (i.e., every social will) confirms and maintains itself and negates opposing wills and their practices—including the will of a totality, an alliance, and the resisting wills of its members, which belong to the nature of being in agreement with oneself; they belong to the nature of concord and convention, custom and legislation, religion and Public Opinion.

[. . .]

11. (The Morality of Religion and the Morality of "the" Public Opinion). [. . .] This consideration leads to the conclusion that whereas religion is associated with conviction and emphasizes morality, Public Opinion focuses on the deed and stresses legality within the larger context of a moral system. Religion wants to dominate the soul, makes the claim for examining the most inner conviction for God's approval, and uses the institution of the confessional to do so. Public Opinion holds to appearances, the obvious and manifest, and therefore is easily and frequently deceived by pretense. It wants the regulated, the regular, and the correct applications of morality and is lazy and indulgent when it comes to excesses of egotism in commerce and trade as long as the law is not openly violated, when transgressions are not made "public," and jail can be barely avoided. Colonial states exhibit such excesses most blatantly. Public Opinion also demonstrates its power in these modern places openly and most freely. An English social politician, Lord Welby (1908, 4), says about the spirit of the United States that "public opinion is lenient, or to say the least, indolent, in its attitude towards unscrupulous greed for wealth. Wrongdoing is too often lightly passed over as *business.* The result is want of confidence in the probity of those who manage great industrial undertakings. Thus the country is predisposed to alarm, and when bad or trying times, come this want of confidence easily degenerates into fright and panic."

[. . .]

13. (The Empirical Characteristics of "the" Ephemeral Public Opinion). The idea of Public Opinion will be examined here separate from its concept by concentrating on its use in everyday language, that is, in its air-like, or gaseous, state. It has the following characteristics.

1. Public Opinion is easily changed; it rises as quickly as it falls because it changes its subjects. Public attention does not devote much time to one subject; it digresses or is diverted. This is especially true of urban Public Opinion, characterized most clearly by the city of Paris, which considers itself the capital of the world, as Rome did. But as the Roman poet admonishes: . . . Nec si quid turbida Roma elevet, accedas, nec te quaesiveris extra! It is an admonition that will be repeated to a turbulent Public Opinion by any thoughtful person. Its variability suggests frequent and sudden changes. What causes it? First and foremost a fact, an event, a success, or a personality, as in "fame makes people change their minds." But also a movement, an agitation, especially under the right conditions. We will meet a classic example, the victory of the Anti–Corn Law League in England, later.

2. Public Opinion is too hasty; like young people, it even displays the characteristics of a child and not necessarily a well-behaved one. Speed and haste are natural and necessary the more Public Opinion is formed

in the city, especially in the capital, where one impression chases the next. Disregarding participation by the masses and focusing on a specific political judgment, even educated individuals by themselves form a "mass" and display its characteristics. One of them, above others, is the ease and speed of excitement, which grows quickly and is reinforced in each individual through an exchange of information. This can be observed in a crowd as soon as individuals come physically close; the larger the crowd, the safer one feels, the more people encourage the individual and increase his passion. Education enables people to feel united in spirit with many others—regardless of physical proximity—and in the knowledge that they are (or are expected to be) comrades in spirit. Thus a specific experience, the impression of an event, will solicit the feelings I hold. This idea affects one's own mental disposition the more one expects everyone to be hit simultaneously, like an electric shock. This is the case in the city, where a rumor or a fact will "spread like wildfire," where at least morning and evening newspapers report the news simultaneously in all parts of the city, if "extras" did not beat them by several hours and customers did not spread the news by word of mouth or by passing on the extra edition.

Opportunities for "private chats" are available, although city dwellers live like strangers among strangers; one meets acquaintances on the train or tramway, at the office, in consulting rooms, in the marketplace or on the streets; one visits friends or one initiates a conversation with a stranger, if the need to talk is strong enough. Everyone "is of the opinion," which is shared by all "decent people." Fast and regular transportation turns the country into something like a city: within twenty-four hours everyone knows the big news and everyone who participates in it is equally moved and affects the general opinion with his own educated opinion.

3. Public Opinion is superficial, which is a consequence of haste and mobility. It acts on appearance and first impression. This impression may be correct and the only plausible one—given that the news on which it is based is true and correct. But often this is not the case. Sayings like *gelogen wie gedruckt* and *gelogen wie telegraphiert* [false like print and false like telegraphed] are expressions of the nineteenth century, a time of awakening for Public Opinion. Telegraphic or printed news becomes unreliable less frequently through a direct lie than through inaccuracy, distortion, conjecture as reality or high probability, addition, or exaggeration. The average educated reader and citizen does not know this or keeps forgetting it. He forms an opinion without examining its reasons. Corrections are ignored or do not penetrate his consciousness.

4. Public Opinion is gullible and uncritical, and more so when a real or an imagined object accommodates its preconceived ideas and opinions,

which are waiting to be fed, even when the subject of opinions is un-
friendly but especially when its wishes are satisfied. The more impatient
the wish, the more gullible Public Opinion becomes.

5. Public Opinion is filled with prejudices that emerge from liquid, and
particularly from firm Public Opinion, that is, from firm convictions and
expressions of the will, dominating ideas and their feelings. They are normally unchangeable when they are based on tradition, absorbed with
mother's milk," received in the earliest and most secure environment
and therefore also natural and evident. This also means that individual
opinions are often only the result of prejudice that resists other ideas and
reasons. There is a contradiction here regarding the first characteristic of
changeability.

6. Public Opinion is persevering and capricious. It gives itself over to
other ideas and lives for the moment, but it bounces back to its more ac-
customed and desired position and does so sooner and more unequivo-
cally, depending on the strength of its prejudice concerning an object or a
personality.

7. Public Opinion is particularly tenacious concerning personalities—
more tenacious than concerning objects—because feelings like joy or aversion are unlimited and connect directly with feelings of good or evil and
favorable or unfavorable expectations that emanate (or seem to emanate)
from a person. The firmer these feelings become, the more Public Opinion
resembles religion again, although the objects of admiration (or fear) are
distinctively different from the usual objects of belief. People are "idol-
ized" or "condemned." This former tendency, in particular, increases after
the death of a person. If, however, such original and genuine religious at-
mosphere lets these departed individuals prevail and continue to be influential—with sacrifices and reconciliation to call on their spirit in times
of distress and danger—Public Opinion will not move far from its basis of
scientific thought. The adoration of a departed hero occurs actually in the
form of a wish, "if only the hero would be (or would have been) among
us," or in the form of a rational thought, "things would have taken another, better course if he had been the leader as commander in chief or
statesman."

8. Public Opinion of the day is under the impressions of the day and
therefore agitated and often passionately moved. It rarely resembles the
idea we have formed of Public Opinion as the mental form of the social,
rational will *(Kürwille)*. But it considers the effect that dominates it unfamiliar and insists on truth and validity as the basis for an opinion. And
more so with reason when it is an expression of a liquid or even firm Public Opinion, since the commotion has settled in these states, and they are
"cooled-off" states that are dominated by rationality, or so it seems. However, it is quite possible that the effect will still be noticeable in them. A

firm "conviction" and a definite opinion—which seem evident to a thinking individual—will not allow one to be "drawn into a fight" by belittling opposing ideas as folly or superstition. It is nothing short of making judgments and actually corresponds to the nature of Public Opinion in its visible firmness. It remains above the hassle of the day and is effective as a collective conviction behind intellectuals—who constitute the republic of the learned. Often it confronts the dominant opinions of the moment, but it is always in danger of being carried away by them. It can be caught up in passion—although this pertains only to the majority of individuals who happen to be the carriers of Public Opinion—since firm Public Opinion is independent of them as free rationality and objective truth; it hovers above the fray and is ready to retreat to a smaller circle of subjects who remain unshakable throughout the storm, like the captain of a ship, more deeply moved by their own ideas, their intention, and their goal than by their surroundings. Genuine Public Opinion as a rational *Weltanschauung* remains, in this sense, above parties and their multiple purposes. The Public Opinion of the day remains always under the influence of firm and liquid Public Opinion, although such a dependence is often obscured and does not exclude contradiction and contrast.

9. According to the ideas of order, law, and morality contained in firm or liquid Public Opinion, air-like Public Opinion is also, in principle, for maintaining these social powers, although it may hardly recognize their nature and is easily agitated by present emotions without realizing the extent of the prevailing ideas contained in them. Morality is the actual arena of Public Opinion—according to our understanding—and one in which it constantly moves around in its diffuse forms. Public Opinion will always pay its respects to morality, although this respect often seems hypocritical, a matter of wanting to look good. Its ideas about morality are colored or distorted by collective interests, party interests, public or national interests of "the" Public Opinion, or the interests of humanity. Thus Public Opinion cannot do without the flag of morality flying in its battles and will grab one along the road where it lies as a "slogan."

10. The Public Opinion of the day is recognized by its use of slogans. "The mother of the slogan is always passion, struggle, and the quarrel of spirits. One examines words like liberalism, progress, the little man, proletariat, press freedom, world politics, revenge, cubism, or naturalism to find that they are or were disputed and embattled. Each one of them becomes a type of 'Gessler's hat' [The *Geßlerhut* in Schiller's drama *Wilhelm Tell*, trans.], erected by the advancing party as a symbol of its power. Like the conqueror who raises his flag over the occupied castle as a sign of his success, slogans are nothing but the banners of those dominant ideas that have just gained some ground" (6).

11. Subject of Public Opinion is the audience as a generalized party, and especially a victorious party, although a slogan is initially taken and used by the political party that fights and wins with it. There are specific opinions about order, law, and morality that emerge in convention, legislation, and finally Public Opinion; they set norms and thus become norms themselves. They are crystallized in slogans, which does not mean that they cannot be taken for being true—for being obtrusive and strong convictions—and that a true Public Opinion could not materialize for these topics to become an irresistible force. They had to grow, they had to be disseminated, and it is not really essential for their success, whether its prophets and proclaimers consciously promote their own interests, class interests or interests of sects, or not. The slogan may be applied in good faith and for its own reasons and be appreciated for its own sake, although there is always the temptation to use it for certain effects. That the speaker knows about its effectiveness is no proof against his own conviction regarding the value and correctness of its ideas. Perhaps he is thoughtless and frivolous to rely foolishly on the goodness of the masses and to resist insights about its real condition. His belief can be similar to a religious conviction. Therefore, it is incorrect and prejudiced to accuse national leaders of demagoguery and of exciting the masses unscrupulously by tossing around slogans. However, the unscrupulous agitator who seeks his own advantage or speaks and works in the service of others may be more successful than the honest enthusiast and idealist. From a historical perspective, nevertheless, and therefore seen objectively, one or the other form of disseminating ideas, beliefs, or opinions is arbitrary and has the same effect. The fact that they are promulgated contains a sociological necessity. The latter is based first and foremost on the results of spreading power, changes in power relations, or a change in the conditions of social power. This is obvious in slogans that embody the ideas of a rational natural law, that is, the convictions of the century of Enlightenment, which triumphed with the French Revolution. "Freedom and equality are proclaimed." [Jacques] Necker, minister and well-meaning reformer, representing the school of enlightened autocracy, wrote about it in 1792 as if it were based on the self-serving intentions of "wire pullers." He says that it was not difficult to lead public opinion, at least not as difficult as producing a constitution. Indeed, the national assembly and its leaders fulfilled the first task better than the second one.

"Especially the opinion of the people is easily subjugated; it is sufficient to know their small number of dominant passions and connect them through real or illusionary means with ideas of how to satisfy them. Individuals of a higher class are often led in the same fashion; they feel flattered to find the indirect reactions of their soul honored with the beautiful name of an idea, reflection, or thought. Therefore, it meant to cleverly serve the constitution by connecting this work with two principles and two words: equality and freedom" (7).

The language itself accentuates Public Opinion. Not only the content but the sound of the words often expresses the emotion that accompanies the imagination served by these words. A word like "freedom" can always count on its magic, whereas words like "usury," "crime," "murder," and the respective identifications of individuals, like "war profiteer" and "black marketeer," are stained and constantly spread by Public Opinion in sayings, anecdotes, and satires.

12. The great weakness of hanging on words, however, is not only a feature of the Public Opinion of the day, but affects also firm and lasting Public Opinion as well as vulgar thought in general. It deals quickly with words, as "young people" do, and is hardly educable when it insists on it. Education and intellectual power are present, but only of an average kind. This level is very different among various circles, groups, and nations. Germans boast with good reason of a relatively high average education. Political education is weak because political interest is not sufficiently developed. Even men with a considerable general education rarely see through the confusion of their own party. Nationalism is vibrant but insights into what is expected from common national interests are weak, and the confusion of national, party, and class interests is a daily occurrence, especially among those who sail under the banner of party and class. "Serious thinkers have a difficult stand vis-à-vis the public." This goes especially for politics, where the public, divided or not, responds to the intellectual with ignorant and naive opinions and prejudices but with great confidence and vehemence. There are certainly reasons to complain and to be angered by the stupidity of Public Opinion. Public Opinion is foolish when it presumes to make a judgment based on superficial knowledge, tendential or incorrect news dissemination, or prejudiced and poorly reasoned opinions—or when the public makes a similar presumption based on its carelessly conceived ideas and imaginations—about topics and questions that require a sharp mind, careful examination, and knowledge of hidden facts and reason—and generally an above-average mind—to be understood.

14. (Emotional politics of "the" Public Opinion). True Public Opinion is the average opinion of many slightly educated and well-informed individuals regarding political issues and questions that accentuate its social power decisively—an average that involves women only marginally—falls behind the concept itself, which demands a well-considered judgment. Emotional politics is the playground of Public Opinion. The former frequently and amazingly encounters planned, rational politics and lends it the valuable support of enthusiasm, even passion, and the ingredients of moral indignation or conviction, which are completely foreign to the

politician as such. But he can use them to justify and sanctify his actions and to bestow a glimmer of virtue and the glow of a religious mission upon them. The art of statesmanship, therefore, involves steering Public Opinion in this sense, or supplying and reinforcing a useful direction, as well as supporting, elevating, and—above all—disseminating it.

[. . .]

Politics will and should be clever, above all; cleverness is intellectual farsightedness, the anticipation of coming events and their effects, the effects of one's own action and inaction, and the moves against one's own moves. The intelligent statesman wants to represent the interests of the state, wants to protect it against damage and provide advantages to improve and secure its position. The more determined he pursues this goal, the more conclusions he will reach regarding what is advantageous, even necessary; but he will fight against the stream of Public Opinion and its emotional politics, because a large segment of an educated public will not recognize or understand his conclusions. A strictly rational art of statesmanship in foreign affairs—guided by scientific thought—will appear weak, fearful, and sometimes compliant and cowardly in the eyes of immature Public Opinion. Such statesmanship will be ready for significant sacrifices in order to reach important goals, especially regarding self-preservation and the survival of the fatherland; such willingness is characteristic for a conscious rational will, which aims for the ultimate advantage and victory. The Public Opinion of a country will resist such sacrifices—particularly if an immediate need cannot be seen—and protest against its incompatibility with the "honor" of the state *(Reich)*.

[. . .]

The statesman, like any other businessman, tends to ignore moral sentiments as required by the absolute pursuit of his goals. Regardless of how difficult or easy it may be to overcome the resistance of his own soul, generally it will be more difficult to overcome the objective power in the form of Public Opinion, especially when the latter coincides with popular belief (8). He must try to weaken this resistance and form it, work on Public Opinion for expediency's sake, or politicize it. Although this may be highly appropriate under certain circumstances, however, it can also be more damaging through the underlying maxim—the weakening of moral feelings. It is certainly true when an attempt is being made to break moral resistance or to behave indifferently toward it or ridicule it; only too often there are bitter consequences, and clever statesmanship must recognize this danger, even when it ignores or ridicules such moral doubts.

Normally, the politics of emotion regarding Public Opinion does not know what it wants; it is frequently filled with contradictions; its logic is a female logic. Thus it is opposed to war with all of its natural and moral aversions triggered by this nightmare, but it insists on a national honor that does not allow softness and is completely upset by the idea of "buying" the goodwill of the enemy with land and rejects such exacting demand as a humiliating practice.

[. . .]

# 5

## Power As a Factor of "the" Public Opinion

### SECTION ONE. POWER

**1. (Innovations).** Indeed, all significant historians praise the fact that Public Opinion—as understood in agreement with the present theory—has played an important role and has demonstrated its power in the critical changes of church and state, legislation, justice, and administration, which occupied the last centuries. This is evident through earlier discussions concerning the states of Public Opinion. In fact, Public Opinion can be understood in terms of its most important claims and accomplishments. It is the modern spirit, the subjective "spirit of modernity," which works slowly, sometimes haltingly or abruptly, develops, and becomes stronger and more successful in destroying and undermining traditional ideas and institutions. It is curious that Public Opinion of the day does not appreciate innovations but rather opposes them and insists that the traditional is valuable and right, perhaps expedient in some cases, and makes good sense in any case. Thus all critical changes of opinions, law, or constitutions were supported by a few or by classes that had not directly participated in the formation of Public Opinion. It was a long historical process, therefore, to invigorate and reinforce Public Opinion, for instance, to come out in favor of free trade, free money markets, and freedom of coalitions and assemblies, in favor of constitutions, voting rights, and their extension; but also against secret and written court proceedings, witch hunts, and torture, and for jury trials and open testimony. In a later phase of development, Public Opinion favored the involvement of the state and law in free labor contracts, limits on private property concerning land and capital, that is, for the legality and expediency of socialistic innovations like legal limits on property rights.

Resistance gathered regularly and most effectively around some religious motives, since religion is a conservative power, not unlike the Public Opinion of the day as long as it remains under its influence. There is always a change, a reformation of Public Opinion that liberates it and puts it on its own feet. It has always been the task of innovators—if they did not appear in the name of a firm or at least liquid Public Opinion—to win it over, or to win over directly the ephemeral Public Opinion of the day. This meant to work on opinions and to change them whenever necessary or possible. The task was performed by single "prophets" with a clear will and supported by a few who—as their followers and apostles—would proclaim the vital truth of their master's message to the world. Also, third persons took over the cause to serve their own advantage and supported and favored the new opinions openly or secretly. The course of the world will be slower and more difficult, the stronger the army of traditional opinions and their concomitant feelings and interests, and the stronger the prejudice and self-preservation of the old order.

In this sense one can observe frequently the emergence of new ideas. Even if they are religious (and sometimes because of it), religion—as traditional, valid, and mostly believed—is a castle to be conquered. Meanwhile, religious ideas struggle with religious, and extra-religious ideas with extra-religious ones. In this case too Public Opinion is on the side of traditional, old, rooted ideas and retreats only slowly under repeated attacks, although occasionally the pressure of a tremendous event will cause a sudden movement toward change. But then there is always a new Public Opinion in place, like the new bearers of sovereign powers who replace the old ones in a political revolution.

[. . .]

# 6

## "The" Public Opinion As a Political Factor in the Life of the State

### SECTION ONE. IN GENERAL AND IN AMERICA

**1. (Recognition of the Fact).** The power of Public Opinion became a solid fact . . . because it was recognized as a factor in the life of the state. It [was] recognized—next to the parliament of a nation—as an institution whose approval or disapproval determines the success of a government measure and therefore its existence and duration. The press and Public Opinion are frequently mentioned together in this context, although the press itself represents an expression or an organ—and lately the most important organ—of Public Opinion. Because of its independent meaning and its power, the press is emphasized and connected to other expressions of Public Opinion, such as conversations, assemblies and their decisions, clubs, petitions, demonstrations, literary publications, theater performances, and so on.

There is also frequent talk of parliament, press, and Public Opinion as a three-part organization of the "people" *(Volk)* or an audience in ways that make Public Opinion the last, deciding institution, because, if unanimous, it determines significantly the position of the press, and even parliament cannot resist it permanently. As soon as parliament is renewed, either in the normal course of events or after its dissolution, new elections are marked by Public Opinion.

In England, for instance, which claims the oldest parliamentary tradition, by-elections are closely observed; thus if the voters of a district produce a majority that differs from the usual (or even the last) election, the results will be interpreted as the sign of an expressed, if not changed, Public Opinion.

In some representations Public Opinion appears as sovereign, as the original, true sovereignty of a really modern state, that is, a democratic state in which the opinion of the majority appears as "the" Public Opinion, which is "the will of the people" *(Volkswille)*. If we strictly differentiate, however, between public opinion and the mood of the people, and "the" Public Opinion and the will of the people, we must recognize that these phenomena merge. Public Opinion frequently affects the mood and therefore the will of the people decisively (or the other way around), with the result that these phenomena cannot be clearly distinguished from each other.

[. . .]

15. (Conclusions). We may conclude that the meaning of Public Opinion as a political factor in the United States is not remarkably different from that in other countries. It is one among other powerful factors, which emerges from "the" society and thus represents the totality of the relevant classes. Public Opinion is there, like everywhere else, the opinion of those who represent education and property, except that there is a stronger emphasis on property. Consequently, "to belong" means to have a considerable fortune or a rather large income, while an average education is quite sufficient and widespread thanks to the formal democracy. Contrasting real plutocracy and formal democracy side by side must be reflected in Public Opinion. The latter is widely extended, and only people of color (Negroes, half-castes, and Indians) and young immigrants are not part of it; their opinions and convictions do not count. Others are second choices: this goes more or less for all non-English Americans, and especially for numerous individual personalities of German-American origin who have been recognized and are appreciated by Public Opinion. The way in which Public Opinion branded them during the war as "hyphenated Americans" is characteristic.

Public Opinion in the United States is Anglo-American. We are thinking only of the fleeting opinion of the day, which is normally understood as Public Opinion. [. . .] Even today the latter is essentially puritan, that is, narrowly petit bourgeois and confiningly religious from its beginnings. But it displays these roots without being restricted to them or believing in them. Public Opinion is externally pious but internally quite secular, and secular in the sense of an Enlightenment thought that considered the Middle Ages only dark. It hardly knows the foundations of its own culture and lives, therefore, more in the present (and in images of the future that are exclusively determined through the present) than Public Opinion in Germany or England, which exists by Goethe's words, "we all live and die by the past."

What we say of Public Opinion in the United States can be said of the "spirit" of Americans because "the" Public Opinion, as we understand it, is the essential expression of a national spirit. There is a gaping contradiction here: it is the late end product of an educational process in Europe that lasted 1,500 years (with reminders of humble churches and few traces of the arts surrounding it), but its spirit is young, its consciousness fresh and quite "rational" in terms of a rationality that is rather preoccupied with the means toward achieving external goals. Thus the American spirit—as it is widely known—is plainly intent on enrichment, making money honestly or dishonestly; Public Opinion approves, even favors it, by admiring wealth, although it demands generous acts of charity, especially support of publicly recognized education. In general, Public Opinion definitely favors the spectacular and is therefore the progressive carrier of modern civilization, which it affirms unconditionally more than any European Public Opinion. The difference between culture and civilization, which recently almost made waves in Germany's liquid Public Opinion, makes no sense in American Public Opinion.

American Public Opinion is individualistic and social; there are no qualitative heights or depths. Adam Smith's observation that everyone is a merchant in American society is valid here more than anywhere else—with the exception of Australia perhaps. According to American Public Opinion, therefore, it is the lifelong task of the individual to engage in business and to do it well and into eternity. Politically this means contempt for the state, while freedom—which had been praised as a result of the progress of civilization—is preferably understood as commercial freedom. A "free reign for the able one" is desirable, but ability is rather seen as smartness, involving slyness and recklessness in pursuit of one's own goals. Public Opinion will not allow this openly but will moralize, although its weakness emerges in the acknowledgment of success, which turns easily into worship of the successful.

The adoration of "freedom" lasted for almost a century alongside slavery. Today there is no conflict with the forms of slave wages, which Public Opinion in Europe would no longer tolerate. The United States is the promised land of capitalism and the middle class, which Public Opinion considers not only a normal but an exemplary condition and the height of human progress. Public Opinion is particularly uncritical of technological progress, which is well favored. But recently this contented Public Opinion lost its firmness and became liquid in some places, when the appearance of corruption and excessive financial power was too obvious for Public Opinion to close its eyes. The influence of an important writer, Henry George, has quietly grown over a generation, it has been noticed, and—together with European socialist and philosophical currents—deconstructs American Public Opinion.

Its uncivilized and ignorant conceit, however, was reinforced again during the world war by English propaganda, which presented Germany as the land of the Huns. Its government—intent on robbery, murder, and arson—would have conquered the world if a noble England would not have come generously and unselfishly to the aid of her beloved French republic, poor little Belgium, and the large and culturally most sophisticated empire of the tsar. The credulous Public Opinion of a superficially educated colony swallowed it all, revealing its emptiness and depravity.

However, there are more genuine parts in the firm Public Opinion of the United States. The fact that a republican constitution and democracy are appropriate forms of a modern state rests on solid theoretical grounds, even while one admits the appalling facts of American political life. The strength of this conviction may be measured by the juxtaposition of the two large parties as republican and democratic; since it is well-known that the Republican Party wants democracy and the Democratic Party the republic, the difference takes on another, original meaning of centralism and federalism. Such a unanimity explains the power of Public Opinion; the masses, regardless of their opposition to the dominant class, share the belief in the republic and democracy. A belief in the monarchy prevails only where it is valued as a tradition and favors a large part of the working people, for instance farmers, or where it fascinated the masses with the glory and victory of war. The industrial worker has been more or less caught up in the enlightenment of an urban existence and is basically republican in outlook. For these reasons domination by the upper class or capitalists is more secure in a republic than in a monarchy, regardless of how a monarchy deals with the demands of the working class.

There is a universal quality in the American working class that is unknown elsewhere when it represents "citizenship" as its strongest element; everyone participates in citizenship. Even though the French language separates *bourgeois* and *citoyen*, the expression remains popular in the contemporary state and even more so in America, since (1) America knows no nobility, no aristocracy (by birth) and thus misses the existing difference between nobility and bourgeoisie elsewhere; and (2) because a large part of the working class, thanks to its rarity in the colonies, has a relatively good income and lives and feels like a petite bourgeoisie. In addition, the adventurous and brave individual has a chance—because of the size of the country and the rapid progress helped by a stream of new immigrants; he does not share the hopelessness of the proletarian in the old countries, who is tied to his fate.

These are the reasons for the impression, described by Bryce, that Public Opinion in the United States is general in nature (indeed, it is) because it is less restricted by class differences than any other European country (but more so by racial differences; characteristically there is no mention of "colored people," although Bryce emphasizes that they have no part in forming the Public Opinion).

A strong aspect of unity is the dependence of a colonial state on the mother country. And despite their variety, American nationals consider Great Britain their motherland, as the seat of their education has always been in the New England states. "The English language has an absolute monopoly in these circles (of the English-speaking world), which amount to over half of the white race. . . ." This monopoly "keeps the Public Opinion of the United States firmly dependent on England, a dependence that is almost as strong as if the States were a British province" (Carus 1916, 23).

[. . .]

# 7

# The Future of "the" Public Opinion

**1. (The Relationship with Religion).** The future of Public Opinion is the future of culture. Undoubtedly the power of Public Opinion is increasing and will further increase. It is also certain that it will be influenced, changed, and occasionally disturbed from below. It makes sense to think of the possibilities for these developments: some will be beneficial, others will be called detrimental by those looking ahead, like the opinions of historians and ethicists about the good and the bad that arises from the shifting effects of Public Opinion. The ways of human civilization regarding the improvement of humankind, whose traces are recognizable through history as we know it, will depend in future centuries on the degree of firmness that Public Opinion will gain in response to ethical questions and on its consciousness regarding such questions.

Although Public Opinion in reality is frequently mixed with religious motives, its form and power are the opposite of the meaning of religion in public life. The Christian religion has lost in later centuries what Public Opinion has gained: there a reduction, here an increase in power and influence. A larger contrast exists between Public Opinion and older, firmer, and more powerful forms of Christianity, like the Roman Catholic Church, than between Public Opinion and the younger, looser, and weaker Protestantism with which it is frequently in close contact—especially in England and the United States—and particularly with dissidents and specifically bourgeois elements. The demise of the Christian religion of any kind will continue, regardless of many noble powers dedicated to its preservation; the self-destruction of Christianity is at work and its regular progression cannot be stopped permanently. Will the result be irreligiosity and the complete decline of morals?

There are close and strong connections between religiosity and morality, but the latter is not essentially determined by religiosity, and even less so by specific types of religion, creed, or dogmatic belief. Public Opinion, however, looks favorably on religiosity (and not only in England and the United States), which it understands as moral seriousness and the relation of life to eternal values. It calls such a sentiment idealism in sharp contrast to "materialism," whose determination is left unclear in a theoretical and practical sense, although its delinquency and falsity are definitive. For this reason, Public Opinion—especially in Germany—has favored a liberally interpreted Christianity as the historical form of moral idealism, which demands neighborliness, gentleness, and sacrifice and is inclined to acknowledge its perfect form of religiosity. But value and meaning, which are part of a belief, are decreasing visibly, and the association of the ideas of Christianity and ethics has become relaxed in the course of the last decades—if observation and experience are correct. In this respect, the conduct among Christian nations had a thoroughly shattering effect, especially how Protestant England and America treated the mostly Protestant Germany with Christian love—beyond the world war itself, since war is a familiar phenomenon for the Christian. After all, its rage contributed immeasurably to the reputation of Christianity; many good and devout Christians defended a just defensive war. But there is hardly anyone who would dare claim the behavior of good Christians as an example of Christianity, like the experience with Anglican clergy and the Baralong murders, or with some German ministers and the regrettable methods justified under international law as reprisals against a hunger blockade.

The retreat to Christian morals is only a cover-up for a position taken by Public Opinion under the influence of the Enlightenment and more fully with the discoveries of the natural sciences and history during the nineteenth century; it is paramount to abandoning the Christian faith. This is a tragic event in the life of peoples for whom the Christian faith meant not only the road to eternal salvation, but also the recognition of metaphysical truths that would reduce rationality and science to lifeless shadows. The conventionality of upper-class society—frightened by the French Revolution and its aftermath when some members sought protection behind the walls of the Church—stopped and delayed this sociological process. But the latter was also slowed down by the monarchistic state and the governments that served it. This impediment has been removed in Germany, Austria, Russia, and in the new national states, as earlier in France and Portugal. Religiosity, even Christianity, can prosper in republican states as well as in monarchies, and the churches can maintain their position, although the conscious support of imagined or real religious ideas and ceremonies by a higher or even the highest authority is gone. Consequently, conventionality is relaxed, although it suffers under the increasing social importance of classes that do not share in it and do not want to be restricted by it. They may have less insight into the conditions and less knowledge, but they feel a stronger need for sincerity and truthfulness concerning questions of existence, which are considered sacred by them. Elements of society with such a background participate more and more in the formation of Public Opinion. The more effective such participation becomes, the less Public Opinion will be restricted by political considerations of any kind. "Without knowing the string, it cannot be undone" (9). People now get to know the string by themselves.

2. (Potential Developments). Several developments are possible. Perhaps a revolutionary development is the most likely one in this case. It already happened once, when fanatical Protestant hordes stormed the pictures and destroyed the magnificent windows of Gothic churches. The grandiose unity of the Roman Catholic Church could have been preserved through reforms and compromises, which would have been infinitely beneficial for the political development of Germany. There are deeper, internal reasons for why it did not happen, which will also necessarily determine the future development. The final crisis of Christianity will be deeper than the crisis of the Church in the sixteenth century. The world will be shaken more deeply.

Another development is equally plausible. The generalization of a free-thinking consciousness, its rise in public opinion, the intensification of its teachings through references to eternity and the infinity of being, and the inexplicability of the nature of things could turn Public Opinion into religiosity. It can constitute the religion of the Holy Ghost, the universal religion of humankind as the fulfillment and perfection of all prior world religions, which thirteenth-century priests anticipated forbodingly. It would be a great victory and triumph of Christianity if it could complete such a process from inside; it would be self-recognition and willpower of Public Opinion, if it would accept and care for Christianity in this sense: not to believe or confess but to fill it with the purest and most genuine intention—the intention to refine humankind.

It is an almost foregone conclusion of Public Opinion that its dominating the economy—a decisive antidote against the power of capital within it—and the rise of labor as a codeterminant factor are prerequisites for improving the public spirit through social reform. Public Opinion does not yet dare approve "socialism," but it does not dare deny it either. It shies away from the word, whose sense is only too closely related to force, bureaucracy, or schematicism, but more so from "communism," which has recently fallen into disrepute through wild movements and language uses. The other word that Public Opinion (at least in Germany) prefers has been mentioned before: "community." During the world war *Volksgemeinschaft* has become, through its accomplishments and its defects, the subject of a consciousness that recognizes the idea of community as reality and moral necessity. It is also recognized that its center is not located in some ideas, theories, and teachings, but in facts, especially healthy family relations, the hearth of genuine morality, which cannot be replaced by the best educational system but only protected and improved by it. The more Public Opinion gathers around this idea, the more it will be able to unite the many powers, different views, and parties toward one goal. True humanitarians have already joined hands without asking for a show of certificates of the correct or corresponding creed and are moving in the direction of measured, feasible reforms of labor laws and land and housing reforms and are moving toward social hygiene in general, including marriage and procreation, and cooperatives that attempt to heal capitalism from within. They are moving against alcoholism, venereal disease, and tuberculosis. The holy ghost of truth, beauty, and goodness is among them—Parakletos, who is called on to strengthen and support everyone. He may be supported by those who confess that it is still more important to hold different beliefs, but one day he will become "the" religion of those who are determined to let only an organically consolidated rationality—using consciousness as its norm—guide their thought and will. Public Opinion becomes the social consciousness, as religion always has been, and the final religion to the degree that it absorbs an ethical content which it will aim to refine.

Thus the future of Public Opinion and the future of culture depend on the future of science. As long as the scientific spirit is brightened and warmed by the flame of truth, it seeks beauty and goodness and their unity. Piety—the sense of respect for the noble which was, which has been sought, and which has been lost—belongs first and foremost to both of them. Humankind could be ennobled if Public Opinion could be taught to cultivate piety and respect, a task related to the education of humankind, according to Goethe, who recognized and proclaimed it.

Science will continue to serve dissolution and destruction. The spirit of truth bears arms rather than a sign of peace. But it also steers the plow and has cultivated much soil; the more its prestige is recognized, the more it will be able to build. And what is built well will last, as new life will rise from the ruins.

3. (The Reform of the Press). Although the future does not comply with our wishes or hopes, in a limited way it yields to our deeds and works, which follow them at least partially. All of us can participate in the formation of the future; we, learned men and women, are especially called upon to participate in the future formation of Public Opinion.

Public Opinion is a form of the intellectual life of a nation—we are thinking here initially of the German nation—and is affected by all elements of this intellectual life, especially science, because it is closest to Public Opinion. All genuine art (which forms taste) lifts the spirit and renews it and therefore (particularly fiction and poetry if they are truly beautiful and noble) may contribute to the education of Public Opinion. Most of these elements are communicated through print; indeed, the idea of Public Opinion is so closely connected with the nature of the daily press that the reform and future of the Public Opinion are inevitably linked to the reform and future of newspapers. Earlier in this work attention has been drawn to old and new accusations against the press, as well as to proposals and suggestions for its improvement.

Finally, I would like to recall the idea of a German American who was inspired during the world war when he suffered heavily under the burden of lies and tough gestures by Anglo-American newspapers during those years. Ferdinand Hansen encourages his fellow citizens to contribute to a $1 billion fund to create a "safety valve" in the public life of the United States "against the selfish power of gold." The goal is the "foundation of a completely independent newspaper in every town, led by experienced, highly educated, and conscientious men—the best heads the country can produce—in connection with pedagogical institutions. Its title will be 'the citizen.'"

> All recognized parties would have free space to follow events and provide comments according to their principles. The voice of the people would find a direct expression. The editorials of the "citizen" would be so colorless, impartial, and objective that their messages or opinions would be received in complete belief, and with the greatest respect and confidence. The newspapers would have their own wire service, free from the lying wires and the poisoned source of Reuters, Havas, Northcliffe, and the yellow financial-imperialistic press. They are the common enemy of humankind, and they must be revealed and destroyed before a real and long-lasting peace and goodwill can rule the world. (Translated from the handwritten original.)

The newspaper must be independent of advertising, or what Hansen calls "the cancer at the heart of all journalism," through large circulation which will be guaranteed by the replacement of newspapers with different party affiliations. "Only reliable companies, respectable advertisers will be given space."

"The depraved and antisocial features of faddish journalism will be resolutely excluded, especially the immoral cloak-and-dagger sensationalism, the shameful violation of the sanctity of privacy, etc." (10).

The basic ideas of this enterprise, applied to American conditions, also have value for us in Germany. We do not think that they will be realized. But they constitute a worthy critique of what really exists in the field of newspaper journalism. The prospects are best—at least in Germany—for a reform from inside by the press, that is, by its most serious and best-educated representatives. The need for such a reform should be set into motion through public opinion, which would be an effective, perhaps the most effective, means of self-education for Public Opinion.

# 8

# Notes and References
## *Kritik der öffentlichen Meinung*

## NOTES

1. After thinking carefully about these differences for five years, I found the following passage in a generally worthwhile book, *Kultur und Presse* by Dr. Emil Löbl. (Max Weber also praised it in his report to the German Sociological Society, Proceedings of the first German Sociological Meeting, Tübingen: Mohr, 1911, 43, as a deserving although relatively little-known book.) After explaining that public opinion will develop and gain power outside and opposite the press, he writes, "The problem will become more difficult since a unified public opinion will be rarer with the growing differentiation and separation of the party system. One can only speak of 'the' public opinion in the case of only one, the only one, or when at least one of several opinions has the overwhelming majority; in all other cases one deals with several different public opinions" (p. 252). Earlier I had become acquainted with the writings of Herbert Jordan [1918]—who died in the war—which appeared fifteen years after Löbl's book, prepared as a doctoral dissertation and posthumously issued by Johannes Hohlfeld, Kamenz, 1918. It states (4): The concept "public opinion" actually is a contradiction per se. The character of the unity—contained in the concept of the subject—is destroyed by the adjective, which points to a multitude of people and, therefore, opinions. Such a combination makes only sense at a time when a people represent an unbroken unity of thought and feeling, or where—as in Romanticism—the concept of a unified and differentiated soul of the people, shaped according to lifestyles, was common and commonly used. In reality, public opinion represents at any advanced stage of development a show of constantly and intensely struggling opposites (especially if the concept is reduced to the political), which are submerged only in the rarest moments in a flood of unanimous feelings. These opposites must be found and represented in their mutual relations of power and tensions." One recognizes how

the young scholar, who sacrificed his life as a real hero, struggles with Löbl's recognized difficulty. To what extent his view must be corrected will be based on what is reported in the text. Jordan calls it a concept, but it is only an idea in the use of language.

2. The defenders of the old church felt already disadvantaged during the time of the German Reformation. They had the Reichsstädte against them, and they had the printing presses. Dr. Eck had to pay for his printing. He wrote to Duke Wilhelm on April 14, 1526, "They are not printing in the Reichsstädte anything against Luther, unless someone does a number of books. Have spent 200 Fl. in six years."

3. See, for instance, Bryce (*Modern Democracies* 2:252): "It must be understood that the public opinion of Australia as a whole, alarmed by the mischief which strikes were doing, and sympathizing with the desire of the wage-earners for a larger share of the products of labour, was generally favourable to the experiment" (of the courts of arbitration, etc.).

4. The importance of drama as a means of agitation and propaganda and therefore public opinion deserves monograph-length treatment to do it complete justice. The role of Beaumarchais's comedy as a thundering warning before the revolution will be recognized in a later context. But there are other interesting examples. The less tolerated open expressions are, the more hidden ones will be applied. In Russia under Nikolas I "art, literature, and poetry were considered the most powerful social levers," and Russia's most important critic, Bjelinski, expressed the view that it is in their very nature. "It appeared neither strange (according to Pypin) to write a play in defense of free trade or a poem to praise a special tax, nor to present the position of the state in a tale while the opponent fought it with a comedy" (Hoetzsch 1917, 63). Also, Schiller's early dramas have the character of an indictment of the powers of his era.

5. It is the contribution of living historians to have suggested the importance of pamphlets and the daily press as evidence of intellectual movement, political controversies, and social development and to have urged their students to study this evidence as indirect historical sources. We gain from these studies a series of useful analyses, for instance, Gustav Körner, *Die norddeutsche Publizistik und die Reichsgründung im Jahre 1870*; Otto Bandmann, *Die deutsche Presse und die Entwicklung der deutschen Frage 1864–66*; Lisa Kulenkampff, *Der erste vereinigte preußische Landtag 1847 und die öffentliche Meinung Südwestdeutschlands*; Theodor Scheffer, *Die preußische Publizistik im Jahre 1859 unter dem Einfluß des italienischen Krieges: Ein Beitrag zur Geschichte der öffentlichen Meinung in Deutschland*; Annie Mittelstaedt, *Der Krieg von 1859, Bismarck und die öffentliche Meinung in Deutschland*. There are earlier independent works on this subject, for instance, by Eduard Cauer, *Über die Flugschriften Friedrich des Grossen aus der Zeit des 7jährigen Krieges*; H. von Zwiedinek-Südenhorst, *Die öffentliche Meinung in Deutschland im Zeitalter Ludwigs XIV*, and many others.

6. Wilhelm Bauer, "Das Schlagwort als sozialpsychische und geistesgeschichtliche Erscheinung," in *Historische Zeitschrift* 122, no. 2: 212–223.

7. *Du pouvoir executif dans les grandes Etats*, 2:266. Wilhelm Bauer has misread this statement when he uses the first sentence of Necker's opinion in his precious and learned book, *Die Öffentliche Meinung und ihre geschichtlichen Grundlagen*, 121.

He wants to demonstrate that the nature and effects of Public Opinion had been recognized by and large. But Necker obviously makes a difference between Public Opinion, which he assigns to "individuals of a higher class" and solemnly calls P. O. an *Opinion du Peuple*. By using quotation marks (which are not in Bauer's citation) he suggests that he means the masses *(Peuple)* rather than the bougeoisie, a difference that arose just at that time. Necker always understands *Opinion publique* as the opinions of the bourgeoisie.

8. G. Maier in his *Ethische Umschau* (May 1915) emphasizes how much statesmen have been influenced by Public Opinion, "which can be quickly and immediately disseminated with the aid of modern means of transportation." Perhaps this explains the fact that the profession of a statesman has become less determinant and that genial statesmen are rare. The codetermination of "peoples" *(der Völker)* contains a great danger because it is more or less arbitrary, anarchic, and mostly determined by the press, whose steady suggestions cannot be resisted by thoughtful and educated individuals. He adds plans for a press reform through its own professional organization. There are similar attempts being made by others.

9. Aristotle's words, used by Höffding [1896] as a motto for the first chapter of his philosophy of religion.

10. See the latest published text, *Zur Frage der Preßreform* by Karl Bücher (Tübingen, 1922).

# REFERENCES

An independent journalist. 1909. "Is an Honest and Saner Newspaper Press Possible?" *American Journal of Sociology* 15, no. 3: 321–334.

Anonymous. 1914. "The Northcliffe Press." *New Statesman*, 18 July, 452–453.

Bandmann, Otto. 1910. *Die deutsche Presse und die Entwicklung der deutschen Frage, 1864–66*. Leipzig: Quellen & Meyer.

Bauer, Wilhelm. 1872. "Das Schlagwort als sozialpsychische und geistesgeschichtliche Erscheinung." *Historische Zeitschrift* 122, no. 2: 212–223.

Bauer, Wilhelm. 1914. *Die öffentliche Meinung und ihre geschichtlichen Grundlagen: Ein Versuch*. Tübingen: Mohr (Paul Siebeck).

Brunhuber, Robert. 1908. *Das deutsche Zeitungswesen*. Leipzig: Göschen.

Bryce, James B. 1921. *Modern Democracies*. New York: Macmillan.

Bücher, Karl. 1922. *Zur Frage der Preßreform*. Tübingen: Mohr.

Buckle, Mém. de Georget II, also, Etudes I n.p., n.d.

Carus, Paul. 1916. "Die öffentliche Meinung in den Vereinigten Staaten." In *Neutrale Stimmen: Amerika–Holland–Norwegen–Schweden–Schweiz*. Edited by Rudolf Euken. Leipzig: Hirzel.

Cauer, Eduard. 1865. *Über die Flugschriften Friedrichs des Grossen aus der Zeit des siebenjährigen Krieges*. Potsdam: Gropius (A. Krausnick).

Feldhaus, Erich. 1922. *Das Deutsche Zeitungswesen*. Leipzig: Reclam.

Höffding, Harald. 1896. *Sören Kierkegaard als Philosoph*. Stutgart: Frommann's Verlag (E. Hauff).

Hoetzsch, Otto. 1917. *Rußland: Eine Einführung auf Grund seiner Geschichte vom Japanischen bis zum Weltkrieg*. Berlin: Reimer.

Jenks, Jeremian W. 1895. "The Guidance of Public Opinion." *American Journal of Sociology* 1, no. 2: 158–169.

Jordan, Herbert. 1918. *Die öffentliche Meinung in Sachsen, 1864–66.* Kamenz: Krausche. Part of his doctoral dissertation, posthumously edited by Johannes Hohlfeld.

Klein. Die Organisation n.p, n.d.

Körner, Gustav. 1908. *Die norddeutsche Publizistik und die Reichsgründung im Jahre 1870.* Hannover: Göhmann.

Kuhlenkampff, Lisa. 1912. "Der erste vereinigte preußische Landtag 1847 und die öffentliche Meinung Südwestdeutschlands." Ph.D. diss., University of Freiburg.

Löbl, Emil. 1903. *Kultur und Presse.* Leipzig: Duncker & Humblot.

Maier, G. *Ethische Umschau,* June 1915 n.p.

Mittelstaedt, Annie. 1904. *Der Krieg von 1859: Bismarck und die öffentliche Meinung in Deutschland.* Stuttgart: Cotta.

Necker, Jacques. *Du pouvoir executif dans les grandes Etats.* Vol. 2. Paris: n.p., n.d.

Ostrogorski, Moisei. 1912. *La démocratie et les partis politiques.* New ed. Paris: Calman–Lévy.

Rogers, James Edward. 1909. *The American Newspaper.* Chicago: University of Chicago Press.

Roscher, Wilhelm. 1908. *Politik: Geschichtliche Naturlehre der Monarchie, Aristokratie, und Demokratie.* Berlin: Cotta Nachfolger.

Ross, Edward A. 1920. *International Ethical Review,* April n.p.

Schäffle, Albert. 1881. *Bau und Leben des sozialen Körpers.* Tübingen: Laupp.

Scheffer, Theodor. 1902. *Die preußische Publizistik im Jahre 1859 unter dem Einfluß des italienischen Krieges: Ein Beitrag zur Geschichte der öffentlichen Meinung in Deutschland.* Leipzig: Teubner.

Sombart, Werner. 1902. *Der moderne Kapitalismus.* Vol. 2, *Die Theorie der kapitalistischen Entwicklung.* Leipzig: Duncker & Humblot.

Stern, Alfred. 1905–1920. *Geschichte Europas Seit den Verträgen von 1815 bis zum Frankfurter Frieden von 1871.* Stuttgart: Cotta.

Tocqueville, Alexis de. 1856. *L'ancien regime et la révolution.* Paris: Michel Lévy frères. The translations were taken from Tocqueville, Alexis de. *The Old Regime and the Revolution.* Vol. 1. Edited by François Furet and Françoise Mélonio. Chicago: University of Chicago Press, 1998.

Tönnies, Ferdinand. 1916. "Zur Theorie der öffentlichen Meinung." *Schmollers Jahrbuch* 40, no. 4: 2001–2030.

Treitschke, Heinrich von. 1917–1920. *Deutsche Geschichte im Neunzehnten Jahrhundert.* Leipzig: Hirzel.

Ward, Lester F. 1919. *Pure Sociology: A Treatise on the Origin and Spontaneous Development of Society.* New York: Macmillan.

Weber, Max. 1911. *Report to the German Sociological Society: Proceedings of the First German Sociological Meeting.* Tübingen: Mohr.

Welby, Lord, 1908. "The American Panic." *Contemporary Review* 93: 1–5.

Zwiedinek–Südenhorst, H von. 1888. *Die öffentliche Meinung in Deutschland im Zeitalter Ludwig XIV.* Stuttgart: Cotta.

# Index

absolutism: enlightened, 143, 173; rational, 145; royal, 142

acclamation, public opinion and, 34

action, opinion and, 38

actually means/actually wants, 117

Adolf, Gustav, 142

advertisements: cleaning up, 153; hidden, 150; monopolies on, 154; withdrawal of, 149

A-forms, 177–78, 180, 181

agitation, 118, 126, 157, 171; drama and, 208n4; opinions and, 93; Public Opinion and, 186–87

Albig, William, 53

*American Commonwealth, The* (Bryce), 26, 35, 106n39

*American Journal of Sociology*, Jenks in, 152

Anderson, Benedict: imagined community and, 41

animal society, 105n23

Anti-Corn Law League, 184

anti-Semitism, 155

applause, expression by, 158

applied research, public opinion in, 73–83

Arendt, Hannah, 104n15

art: Public Opinion and, 175; religion and, 161

assembly: ideal/real, 134, 135–36; parliamentary, 136; public opinion and, 136; right to, 34

attitudes: behavior and, 4; as mediators, 38

audience, 133; dispersed, 3, 68, 125; gathered, 125, 171

Augustenburg, Duke Friedrich Christian von, 145

August, Ernst, 140

banquets, 163

Baralong murders, 202

Barth, Theodor: on newspaper companies, 150

basic law (1833), 140

Bauer, Wilhelm, 11, 19, 32, 58, 90, 163–64, 165; criticism of, 81; on individual opinions, 36; on Necker, 208n7; on newspapers, 81; opinion of the public and, 81; on public opinion/expression, 156, 157–58, 160–61; sensationalism and, 100; writings of, 114, 160–63

Beaud, 15; on common opinion/public opinion, 42

Becker, Robert Howard, 103n12

behavior: attitudes and, 4; decisive predispositions toward, 38

being together (*Zusammen-Wesen*), 179

beliefs: opinion of the public and, 66; orthodox/heterodox, 141; popular, 66, 190; rationality/logic and, 178

believing, 21, 117, 118; opining and, 62, 84

211

# About the Editors

**Hanno Hardt** is John F. Murray Professor of Journalism and Mass Communications and professor of communication studies at the University of Iowa, and professor of communications at University of Ljubljana, Slovenia.

**Slavko Splichal** is professor of mass communications and public opinion at the University of Ljubljana and director of the European Institute for Communication and Culture.

**Gary T. Marx** is professor emeritus at the Massachusetts Institute of Technology.